SCZ

D0200401

2007
5X 12/09 · 2/10
11X 4/11 8/11

Bit Literacy

01000010011010010111010000100000
01001100011010010111010001100101
01110010011000010110001101111001

Bit Literacy

Productivity in the Age of
Information and E-mail Overload

By Mark Hurst

Good Experience Press

Table of Contents

The Buddha resides quite as comfortably in the circuits of a digital computer or the gears of a cycle transmission as he does at the top of a mountain.

— Robert Pirsig, *Zen and the Art of Motorcycle Maintenance*

Preface

I was five years old when I first encountered the digital world. It was 1978, and I was in kindergarten in Subic Bay, Philippines, during my father's Pacific tour as a naval officer. One day my teacher welcomed a guest speaker to the class, a uniformed marine who carried in a strange, TV-like box and set it on a table. We gathered around, peering at the glowing screen. I was transfixed. Every few seconds, colored blocks appeared all over, in random places. The marine told us to touch the screen.

My classmates and I each put a finger somewhere on the screen. We waited for the computer to refresh the pattern of blocks, and the moment it did, I saw a brightly colored rectangle sitting directly underneath my index finger. It was a strange and exhilarating moment; how had the computer known I was waiting for it, then and there, to appear?

It was only a trivial computer program intended for the class demonstration, but for me it created a pivotal moment. I could feel that I was touching something more than a screen, more than some glowing filaments. I felt a connection—almost physically— to something deeper, beyond the screen, that was dynamic and responsive, almost alive. So began my lifelong fascination with digital technology.

I grew up during a formative time for the technology industry and became familiar with many kinds of computers, video games, and other digital devices. But by the time I went to MIT to study computer science, something new and different was taking shape: the Internet. Within a few years I witnessed the spread of e-mail and the Web to people all around me—family, friends, and classmates—who quickly adopted the new tools into their lives.

Today hundreds of millions of people around the world are online, using millions of websites and applications and over a billion e-mail addresses. Computers, cameras, cell phones, PDAs, and a menagerie of other devices connect people to each other across the network, and data floods from device to device in an unending torrent, for an infinite variety of uses: e-mails, phone calls, photos, videos, meetings, classes, games, music, and on and on and on. All of the data is made of nothing but tiny electrical impulses, signifying 1s and 0s: these are bits, short for "binary digits."* Everything digital, everything you see and read and use on a computer or digital device, is made of bits: e-mails, Web pages, computer graphics, spreadsheets and documents, downloaded music, everything.

The popularity and easy access of bits, thanks to the Internet, have created both an opportunity—for new experiences and tools and services—and a new crisis. People are overloaded by too many bits, everywhere, all the time. I've noticed in recent years that most people don't know how to deal with the constant deluge of bits, and they suffer as a result. Millions of people are living with stress, working less productively, and feeling the effects in their personal lives. I've met my share of these people in meetings, at conferences, and in airports—all rushing to their next appointment, paying attention only to their e-mail, or cell phone, always with an anxious, distracted look; too busy to talk, or to think, let alone enjoy life. Meanwhile, the problem is growing: there are more e-mails, more bits of all types, coming at them all the time. For the sake of these people, their families, their employers, and the larger economy, there *has* to be a better way.

There is a better way. It's something I call "bit literacy," a set of skills for living and working with bits in a healthy and productive way. Bit literacy can work for any user, in any occupation, at any age, using any kind of computer, under any load of bits. It just requires

---

* The American mathematician and engineer Claude Shannon pioneered methods of encoding and transmitting digital data, which made the Internet possible. He mentioned "bits" in a 1948 paper, though according to Wikipedia, he credited statistician John Tukey with coining the word.

learning and practicing some basic skills. Much like literacy itself, bit literacy can grant a lifetime of benefits, and it doesn't require any special software or expensive tools. The basic principles apply to any situation and any technology where bits appear.

The importance of such skills in today's world cannot be overestimated. Bits are everywhere, and they're increasing every day; they have changed the world like no other technology since perhaps the invention of paper. This is no longer the industrial age, the atomic age, or the space age. We are now living in the age of bits. Those who know how to work with bits will master the age; those who don't will be left further and further behind in every profession and creative pursuit that bits infiltrate.

This book is an invitation to take control of your bits by learning the methods and skills of bit literacy. The skills are yours to learn and use; no software, website, or device can do it for you. I've designed the book to make it as easy as possible to understand why and how to start practicing bit literacy. Chapter 1 starts with a description of bits and their unique qualities that give rise to such dramatic opportunities, and problems. Chapter 2 explains why it's your responsibility to practice the solution; and Chapter 3 describes the solution itself: emptiness. In a phrase, bit-literate users must "let the bits go."

Chapter 4 begins "The Method," a set of chapters describing the major skills involved in bit literacy: managing e-mail, todos, media diet, and photos; creating bits and choosing the right file formats for them; and naming and storing files. Chapter 12 lists other essential tools and skills that practitioners should learn, and finally in Chapter 13, "The Future of Bit Literacy," I describe why I think practicing the discipline will become increasingly important. Technically-minded readers, whom I call "techies" throughout the book, may also like to read the appendices. Appendix A encourages developers to create more bit-literate tools; Appendix B gives my answer to the "Mac vs. Windows" debate and describes how my company sets up employees' computers to enable bit literacy.

Acknowledgements

I owe thanks to many people who helped make this book possible. First and foremost I want to thank Phil Terry, my friend and business partner in two companies and many projects, for encouraging me from the beginning to develop this method, teach it to him and others, and write the book.

Thanks also to Richard Saul Wurman. His influential and prescient book *Information Anxiety* helped me better understand the problem of overload; it remains relevant today, almost twenty years after it was published. The words "bit literacy" first appeared in print in an essay I wrote for Wurman's sequel book, *Information Anxiety 2*. (Thanks to Nicholas Negroponte for introducing me to Richard.)

Thanks to the readers of my Good Experience newsletter, and the goodexperience.com website, who over the years have read and commented on my occasional writing about bit literacy. Thanks also to the attendees of my Gel conference for letting me float my ideas from the stage. Special thanks to the early users of Gootodo.com for taking the plunge before this book was even announced.

Thanks to friends and colleagues who advised me along the way: Dawn Barber, Zimran Ahmed, Laurea de Ocampo, Seth Godin, Karen Watts, David Bodanis, Phil Mirvis, Ellen Stephen, Scott Heiferman, Andrew Zolli, Andrew Rasiej, Phoebe Espiritu, Paul and Cody Phillips, and especially Stephen Bauman. Thanks to the Creative Good team and the Gel team for always doing outstanding work, and for enduring the time I spent away from other duties to write the book. And thanks to the great Cat Fitzgerald for her support and encouragement of these ideas for so many years.

Thanks to my entire family, from Virginia to Georgia, and from Pennsylvania to California to Indonesia, for their love and support. I want to especially thank my parents for those blessings.

Finally, thanks to my wife, Ali, for all her patient listening and expert editing. She's my strongest supporter, my muse, and the love of my life.

Part I | **The Context**

Chapter 1: **Bits**

Bits are heavy. Though they have no physical weight, bits—the electronic data that flows in and out of our e-mail inboxes, cell phones, Web browsers, and so on—place a weight on anyone who uses them. A laptop computer weighs the same few pounds whether it holds one e-mail or a thousand, but to the person who has to deal with all those e-mails, there is a big difference. Appearing in large numbers as they often do, bits weigh people down, mentally and emotionally, with incessant calls for attention and engagement.

Bits are appearing everywhere today, and people are feeling the strain. E-mail traffic has increased, computers and other devices have proliferated, new acronyms and technology terms have invaded our speech, and many people can sense that there's a problem. It's all too much. "Information overload" is discussed at the water cooler, bemoaned in the press. The global economy is full of overloaded workers who are more weighed down, less productive, and ultimately less happy as human beings because of too many bits, and no solution for dealing with them. From CEOs to schoolteachers, designers to doctors, students to retirees, millions of people around the globe have an immediate need to solve their bit overload.

The problem can be solved by learning bit literacy, a new set of skills for managing bits. Those who attain these skills will surmount the obstacles of overload and rise to the top of their professions, even as they enjoy a life with less stress, greater health, and more time for family and friends. Bit literacy makes people more effective today, even as it equips them for the future.

But most users have no idea that they need to learn new skills, since they already know how to use the computer. For a long time, users have only been taught "computer literacy," the set of common actions in software: clicking buttons, selecting menus, opening and closing files. These skills were sufficient in the pre-Internet world of the 1980s, when computers were mostly used as glorified typewriters. But those skills are sorely inadequate in the age of bits. That old worldview is obsolete.

Today the computer and all its software are much, much less important than the bits that they operate on. Bits, after all, are no longer caged inside the computer. They flow—from computers to other computers and devices of all kinds, surging across the Internet in wild arcs at every moment; flowing out of computers, out of cameras, out of phones, out of PDAs, and into inboxes, onto Web pages, onto hard drives, momentarily at rest, awaiting their next trip across the world. Bits, not software, are what's most important today.

The world has changed, but most people haven't caught up yet. Millions of technology users are trying to survive in the new world of bits with only the skills of computer literacy. They know how to send an e-mail and print a document, but they're powerless against the avalanche of incoming bits. Without managing their bits, users are constantly buried; not because bits are a bad or destructive force (far from it), but because users aren't applying the right skills or the right mindset.

Despite having occupations outside the technology field, many people are finding their daily work and life greatly affected by their relationship to bits. I recently met a woman who works as an analyst for a large non-profit organization, focusing on global poverty. She is well outside the technology field, and yet she constantly feels distracted and overloaded by bits. She told me that she feels the need to check e-mail whenever she gets home from work, and on weekends and vacations, too. Her case is not unusual. Bits have invaded practically every occupation, nearly every aspect of communication, commerce, logistics, and entertainment. Bits have arrived, they're not going away, and we must learn how to live with them.

Some people mistakenly try to engage all the bits, all the time, with an "always-on" lifestyle. For example, a familiar sight in airports these days is Busy Man. He's the one with the latest device in hand, scrolling through messages, or barking into a cell phone as he dashes through the terminal, oblivious to everyone and everything around him—the picture of stress and anxiety. On some level, Busy Man likes acting this way because it proves he's important. The more bits he drowns in, the more urgent his work becomes; and urgency, to him, equates to importance. It also offers him a good excuse if he misses a meeting or acts rudely—he was "maxed out," after all, when it happened. Despite how it may appear, working in such a way is neither effective nor sustainable. Urgency and haste are not the way to manage bits properly.

Other people react passively to the influx of bits in their lives, perhaps not even aware of it as an issue to address. No one taught them differently, so they can't be blamed for acquiescing, idly watching their inbox fill up with thousands of e-mails. But passivity is not a solution. As bits accumulate, the user gradually begins to feel out of control, never quite caught up. More bits demand more time and attention: more e-mails to scan, more websites to read, more files cluttering the desktop. And so the user, feeling overloaded with work, begins to hand over some family time to the bits—checking e-mail during dinner, twiddling the BlackBerry during the kids' soccer game.

For both Busy Man and the passive user, the problems stem from not knowing or acknowledging the weight of bits. Bits are heavy whether you consume too many or try to ignore them. They have other attributes, too, that are worth knowing. These attributes reveal bits to be a brand new material, bringing with them new challenges and opportunities. Like paper, or steel, or gunpowder, bits must be fully understood, and respected, if they are to be used to any advantage.

As a comparison, consider the qualities of paper, the material that bits are often meant to replace. Paper has been carrying data for thousands of years, plenty of time for people to understand its many advantages, like low cost and durability. A spiral notebook—bought for a few cents—can hold a stack of handwritten notes, and yet if it's dropped on the floor, the words stay on the page (unlike, say, a document on a laptop). What's more, the paper can remain intact for decades or more, never needing an upgrade. Paper requires no energy source but ambient light for readability.

Paper also occupies physical space, which allows for an elegant "user interface": turning pages and writing words are easy and intuitive, and accompanying technologies like staples and bookmarks are always compatible. Physical size gives paper another benefit: overload is hard to ignore. A big stack of reports, bills, or magazines may sit in plain sight on a table, or a desk, until it's carried away—at which time the physical weight gives another reminder of its quantity. Overload by paper is certainly possible, but at least it is accompanied by familiar real-world properties.

An obvious disadvantage of paper, though, is the time, energy, and material it requires for production and transportation. Paper is a very particular blend of atoms: some harvested from trees, others synthetically made and slathered on as inks and glues. The resulting combination (a stack of newspapers, say) requires yet more expensive atoms, to burn as fuel, in order to move the vehicle carrying the paper atoms to their destination.

Bits are different from paper in almost every way. For one thing, they don't kill trees. Although computer hardware can be poisonous to the environment, the bits themselves are just made of electrons: tiny impulses with no physical weight, taking up no appreciable space. This is an amazing benefit: a practically infinite amount of information can be stored without any increase in physical space or weight! And transmission speeds allow bits to travel across the world within seconds, powered only by the electricity required to send the signal. It's easy to create large quantities, too. With a single click, an e-mail newsletter or website update can reach hundreds of thousands of people in seconds—no printing press or delivery truck required. And once in the e-mail inbox, or on the Web page, the bits will display exactly the same words and graphics, in exactly the same colors, year in and year out, never fading, until they're deleted.

Bits have unique properties, then, that we can use to our advantage: they're super-small, super-fast, easily acquired and created and copied and shared in near-infinite quantity, protected from the ravages of time, and free from the limitations of distance and space. In practice, though, bits reveal several paradoxes: they're weightless, but they weigh us down; they don't take up any space, but they always seem to pile up; they're created in an instant, but they can last forever; they move quickly, but they can waste our time.* Avoiding or ignoring these paradoxes inevitably brings on overload; bit literacy teaches you how to accept and work with them, in order to take control of your bits.

---

* Compared to the wide organic diversity of atoms, which come in all sizes and configurations, bits are limited to two states: 1 or 0, on or off. Maybe it's the close proximity of opposites that causes such frequent paradox in the bit world.

Chapter 2: **Users**

Many people know they're overloaded. What they may not realize is that they're responsible for their own success in managing their bits. To be free of overload and the problems it causes, users must *choose* to become bit-literate. This is more than making a mental decision to change; it requires actively working with bits in a new way. Learning the necessary skills isn't difficult, but it can be a barrier for many people.

The great majority of users are comfortable with technology only within a familiar territory of common programs and features. Their work habits are sufficient to the tasks at hand, which are all they feel they can handle. To these users the prospect of reaching any further to improve their skills can seem daunting, beyond their capacity. I've often heard people say apologetically that they're "not a computer person," as though they possess some innate shortcoming that prevents them from working productively with technology. This is unfortunately a common misconception. It's the poorly designed tools that people are forced to use, and a lack of bit literacy training, that conspire to make things so difficult.

Other users are more confident in their abilities, and know they could change if they wanted to, but perceive that they don't have enough time to do so. They continue to play Busy Man, or Busy Woman, loaded down with bits, hoping that they can catch up if they run just a little faster. Taking a moment to learn new skills seems far too expensive an investment, even if the results are immediate and last a lifetime.

As different as they are, both types of users have something in common: they live by reaction, never taking an active role in managing their bits. Whether floating along or rushing around, they're trapped in a continuously overloaded state, living at the whim of technology, and too intimidated or busy to do anything about it. Besides, most people see it as the job of the technology industry to make them more productive. They await an external solution to their overload.

Seeing this as a market opportunity, the technology industry enthusiastically sells promised solutions to the problem. Overload is a technology-related problem and thus, goes the pitch, the solution must be yet more technology. "Leave it to us," the industry says to users. "Buy our tools, and all their many upgrades, and we'll take care of you." Those who have faithfully upgraded any software tool over the years can judge for themselves whether the tech industry lives up to its promises.

Although we need hardware and software to work with bits, no technology company has the solution to bit overload. It's far too rarely stated that the technology industry is not in the business of making people productive. It is only in the business of selling more technology. Granted, some companies make better tools than others, and users can be productive with some of today's tools. But in the technology business, users' productivity is secondary to profitability. No matter what a company claims, feature lists and upgrades are designed for the company's success, not the users'. This isn't a judgment against technology companies; to the contrary, they are a vital part of the economy and do the world a service by creating new and useful innovations. The point is merely that users should not look to the technology industry to deliver the solution to their overload. Doing so cedes control to companies that, whenever they have the choice, would rather have paying customers than productive customers.

Users themselves, and no one else, are responsible for their success with bits. The only way to guarantee your own productivity is to manage it yourself.

Taking responsibility for your own success is an essential step toward bit literacy, just as important as acknowledging that bits are heavy. It's a conscious decision that requires a Copernican change in perspective: technology should revolve around the user, not the other way around. Yes, tools are essential; but the most effective user is the one who can use her tools freely, in whatever way is best for her, rather than being locked in to any company's offerings. It's more difficult to achieve this freedom, since it's easier just to buy and use whatever the technology industry sells us, but it's ultimately more rewarding.

Bit literacy is an invitation to all users to take control of their bits and become as effective as they want to be. It does require some time and effort, but it doesn't require high-tech aptitude—you don't need to be a "computer person"—and it doesn't require expensive software. While it helps to be able to choose one's tools, even users in the largest corporations, on company-issued computers, can become fully bit-literate. Senior citizens going online for the first time can become bit-literate. Perhaps most importantly, young children who are developing lifelong habits can and should learn these skills. The way they work with bits will define their lives and careers to a greater extent than any previous generation.

The only people who may find these skills irrelevant are those who worship technology for its own sake. These include Busy Man, who shows off the latest upgrade as a symbol of his success, and many techies who are simply in love with technology. For them, productivity isn't nearly as interesting as endlessly examining and comparing the tools and features that promise it. Trendy buzzwords and fads, leading-edge features, and above all, complicated frameworks and systems: these are the things worth playing with and blogging about. To such people bit literacy may seem hopelessly out of step with the times, too simple to bother with.

But simplicity is exactly what bit literacy offers. Users who practice it will find that they become *more* productive than those who try to keep pace with the technology industry. The difference comes from users choosing to be in control of their bits, rather than ceding that responsibility to the tools.

Chapter 3: **The Solution**

Bits are heavy, and it's the users' responsibility to manage their bits in order to avoid overload. But how? The core of bit literacy is a simple solution, applicable in every situation where bits appear, requiring no conceptual leap or complex framework. In fact, it's really the only possible logical conclusion.

Let's review. Bits are overloading users from all sides, constantly, and they're increasing. The overload makes users less productive and more stressed; thus, there's a need for some solution. Passively ignoring the problem won't work, since bits are still heavy, even if we pretend not to notice. And rushing around trying to react to all of the bits at once doesn't work; Busy Man isn't effective, healthy, or sustainable. The solution must lie outside those two strategies, and it must work at any scale. Bits are now essentially infinite, since any amount of load we manage today will be exceeded tomorrow. The solution, therefore, must be both effective and sustainable, indefinitely, in a world of infinite bits. There is only one possible solution.

Let the bits go.

The key to managing and thriving in a world of infinite bits is to let the bits go. This deserves some clarification, because the phrase is easily misinterpreted. First, it doesn't mean to delete everything—hardly an effective strategy. I once gave a seminar in which an attendee told me that she has an easy way of dealing with her incoming e-mail: whenever her inbox gets too full, she simply "lets the bits go" by deleting all the messages. Important or not, read or unread, everything simply disappears, never to bother her again. When I expressed some concern about her method, she replied, "Oh, if it's really important, they'll write back."

There's another possible misinterpretation of "let the bits go," and that's not to use bits at all. Live off the grid with no e-mail, no cell phone, no digital camera, no Internet access at all. Such a lifestyle might be appropriate for some people, but not for anyone who needs to work with digital technology. Bit literacy means engaging the bits, just as any discipline requires meeting the challenge, or the material, at hand. Meditation means wrestling with one's own distracted mind; painting means picking up a paintbrush; bit literacy means engaging the bits.

Bit literacy doesn't even mean that you should engage fewer bits. To the contrary, the goal is to free users so they can engage as many bits as they want, and yet never feel overloaded. The actual quantity of bits you engage, whether it's higher or lower from one day to the next, is immaterial. The important thing is to learn how to engage the bits appropriately—to do the right thing with the bits at the right time. To rephrase Ecclesiastes, there's a time to save, and a time to erase; a time to turn on, and a time to turn off; a time for all actions. But one must always look for ways to let the bits go. There is no other way to work in a world of infinite bits.

I sometimes demonstrate bit literacy in seminars by drawing on a whiteboard. I draw a square with nothing inside, just blank white space. Then I write a word in the box. There was nothing in the square before, and now there's one thing in it. The word is plainly visible.

Then I draw another square, the same size as the first. I use the marker to color in the entire box, so it's all ink and no whiteboard showing. Then I ask everyone: what's the best way to transmit a message in this environment? If we produce a new word, what happens? I write a word in the square, and it's invisible. It's just ink on more ink—there's too much ink already, and no contrast, to show what or where the word is. I can write more words, but as much as I try to write, still no message is transmitted. The environment is saturated with information and further writing does nothing. What, I ask, is the solution?

A clever student knows the answer right away: grab the eraser. If I take the eraser to that second square, completely saturated by ink, I can finally communicate in the noisy environment by taking away some of the material inside. I can write a word with the eraser; or I can erase a section of the whiteboard, allowing me to write new words in that space; or I can erase the entire square interior, allowing the reader to focus completely on the next word that's written there.

When bits are infinite, the only way to thrive is to pick up the eraser. This is letting the bits go: always looking for reasons to delete, defer, or filter bits that come our way. Anything else allows the bits to pile up. Success comes when we get the square empty. Thus another way of describing bit literacy is the constant attempt, in a world of infinite bits, to achieve emptiness.*

Emptiness is at the heart of bit literacy, and that may be an unsettling idea. Emptiness often has negative connotations: "I got nothing out of it." "This is leaving me empty." We prefer to have something. We live in a culture, after all, where more is better. The symbol of success is abundance, measured in size and quantity: bigger houses, for example, containing more stuff. This isn't a moral judgment but merely a point about acquisition. In a world where resources are finite, or scarce, people are often evaluated by how much stuff they have.

Things are different in the bit world, where size and quantity don't mean much. Bits are abundantly available to anyone with Internet access. Like the ink in the colored square on the whiteboard, the challenge isn't getting more; it's making sense of it all, in spite of the glut. The scarce resource is not the bits but our time and attention to deal with them. Success in the bit world comes from creating a quiet, empty place where we can focus on the bits we want, when we want them.

---

* Fans of *The Matrix* will remember what Neo says at the climactic point of the movie, when he achieves his full power in the bit world: he says "no."

Emptiness brings with it one immediate benefit: relief. I call it being "done," a state that many people haven't experienced for many years, if ever. Growing up I had a ritual on the last day of school for just this purpose. After I returned home from the final class, I would throw all my folders and papers into the backyard grill and light a match. There was something freeing about seeing all the projects and papers disappear into smoke. Summer had officially started, and I was *done*. No more class assignments, no more burden of long-term projects, and no worries about where to store the old papers. I was done because I had let it all go.

Today it's harder and harder to be done. Just as we answer one e-mail, two more come in; just as we finish one project, we're reminded that another is behind schedule. We only partially listen to the music or watch the video we just downloaded, because we're too busy downloading another to put in the queue. Bit literacy grants the possibility of being done—not just occasionally but on a regular basis—in order to work more productively and enjoy a fuller life outside of work.

The next several chapters describe the method for achieving emptiness (and productivity) in each of our major incoming "bitstreams"—e-mails, todos, newsletters, photos, and so on. In each case, the method shows how to let the bits go, thus avoiding overload. Later chapters discuss how to create bits most effectively, so as to avoid overloading the recipients of those bits.

One other component to bit literacy is learning to work appropriately with tools. Tools mediate our engagement with our bits, so efficiency is essential. The faster we are with the tools, the sooner we can be done, and the more time and energy we'll have for more important things. After all, our jobs are not simply to manage bits. Instead, it's only when we let the bits go—when we achieve emptiness—that we can begin to think clearly and work more effectively. Bit-literate users must constantly look for the simpler tool, the faster method, the easier interface. Thus the final chapters discuss how to work with today's tools in a way that lets the bits go with the greatest efficiency.

Part II | **The Method**

Chapter 4: **Managing Incoming E-mail**

The first skill to learn in bit literacy is managing incoming bits, and the most important bitstream to manage, for most users, is e-mail.

There is a simple solution to e-mail overload: don't become overloaded. After all, it's only logical that if overload is the problem, then removing the load is the solution. Bit literacy means letting the bits go; anything else perpetuates the problem. Consider what happens when the e-mail inbox is full of messages—dozens, hundreds, or thousands. The overload makes the user less effective in several ways:

- It takes longer for an overloaded user to reply to an incoming e-mail. Each new e-mail that arrives is in competition with the swarm of e-mails already clamoring for the user's attention. The higher the message count, the less chance any given e-mail will get a timely response. What's worse, it's more likely that the user will leave something important undone.

- Prioritization is difficult. Even if the user knows which few messages are the most important, the inbox isn't built to display them in that order.

- It takes longer to find a specific message in a crowded inbox. Even searching and sorting may not help much, since (for example) many messages from the same person, with the same Subject line, could all be sitting in the inbox.

- It's hard to remember which e-mails say what, requiring the overloaded user to open and read the same messages multiple times—an inefficient and demoralizing process.

– An overloaded user cuts into the productivity of others, since colleagues may have to send extra e-mails to remind the user what he's left undone. This adds yet more e-mail to the user's bulging inbox and makes no friends around the office.

– In Microsoft Outlook and other software-based e-mail programs, especially large inboxes are more likely to crash, losing all contents.

The problems don't stop there. There are also psychological costs to a bulging inbox:

– Overloaded users are never sure whether they're forgetting something important buried in the inbox, and so they live in fear of being "found out" or punished for what they forgot. This fear only compounds their feelings of guilt and stress, making them even less effective at managing the problem.

– A full inbox showing weeks or months of old work constantly reminds the user how far he is from being "done." Dealing with old messages often requires the unpleasant step of admitting one's mistake and apologizing for being so late.

E-mail load is measured by the number of messages sitting in the user's inbox. Inboxes containing one or two *thousand* e-mails aren't uncommon in the business world, and yet many users who carry such a load still claim that they feel fine. (The biggest message count I've ever heard, and I'm not making this up, was 150,000. That user said he did *not* feel fine.) There are several reasons why many people end up overloaded by e-mail.

Some users seem to enjoy having lots of messages. Like Busy Man, they grow accustomed to the feeling of urgency from having so many e-mails to react to. In fact, a bulging inbox can be a perverse source of pride. It "proves" that they're important—that is, more important than their colleagues—and gives an excuse for their confused, rushed behavior. Such people are of course the least effective, since they spend their time scrambling and can't work or think clearly.

For other users it can feel lonely not to have at least some e-mails in the inbox, constantly calling for their attention. "E-mails are sort of like friends," someone told me once. "I'll miss them if they're all gone." Having no e-mails forces the user to get on with real work—as managed by the todo list, described in the next chapter—and doing work is hard. It's easier to stay distracted by the messages in the inbox, so as to avoid more demanding activities.

The most common reason for overload, however, is that people often use the inbox for purposes it wasn't designed for:

– *Todo list:* Users often keep action items in the inbox. Buried under other messages, they're hard to find and easy to forget.

– *Filing system:* Meeting notes, project status messages, attachments containing proposals, and other important documents often sit in the inbox, instead of going to a proper project folder.

– *Calendar:* Dates and times for meetings, conference calls, and other appointments pile up in the inbox, often sticking around long after the appointment has passed.

– *Bookmarks list:* Some e-mails remain in the inbox because they contain Web addresses, or usernames and passwords for website logins, that the user isn't sure where to store.

– *Address book:* Messages containing phone numbers and postal addresses of contacts sit in the inbox instead of being entered into an actual address book.

It's a mistake to rely on the e-mail inbox for *any* of these functions. The inbox is appropriate only as a temporary holding place for e-mails, briefly, before they're deleted or moved elsewhere. Here it's important to distinguish between e-mail and what it communicates. E-mail is just a medium; the *content* determines what the message truly is and where it belongs. Users should use the right tool for each kind of message: a todo list for todos, a calendar to store appointments, and so on. No message, no matter what it says, belongs in the inbox.

The inbox is like the sorting room at the post office, where envelopes come in bearing different messages and are quickly whisked away to the right place. Or consider that an incoming e-mail has the shelf life of Chinese takeout in the refrigerator. It's best to eat it as soon as it arrives; within a day is OK, but after that it starts to get funky. Now imagine a refrigerator full of thousands of takeout containers, some of them years old. Like a misused inbox, it's unsafe for new additions and unpleasant to deal with.

The solution

The solution to e-mail overload lies in addressing the root of the problem: the number of current distractions. Every e-mail staring us in the face is competing for our attention with every *other* e-mail we have. An inbox bulging with messages is demoralizing because it reminds us how much work we still have to do, and how far behind we are in doing it.

E-mail load is often measured, inaccurately, in terms of message volume. Whenever people complain that they get fifty or a hundred messages a day, they're talking about their volume—the number of daily incoming messages. But volume isn't an appropriate measurement of load, since it says nothing about how many *other* messages are still awaiting their attention. As stated earlier, the correct way to measure e-mail load is by the message count, the number of e-mails currently sitting in the inbox. Someone with a high e-mail volume—a hundred messages a day or more—may not be overloaded at all, if their message count is low. Conversely, a user who gets only ten e-mails a day may still be painfully overloaded, if their message count is high.

Remember the guiding premise: if overload is the problem, then removing the load is the solution. This has little bearing on e-mail volume, since for the most part, users can't control how much e-mail they receive.* Rather, the solution has to do with message count. Put plainly, here is the solution to e-mail overload:

Empty the inbox at least once a day.

In other words, clear out incoming e-mails before they pile up too high in the inbox. Delete most of them, file some of them (as described in the chapter on storing files), but most importantly, get them all out of the inbox before they become stress-inducing distractions. This is consistent, by the way, with the key ideas of the first three chapters:

1. "Bits are heavy": a bulging inbox demoralizes users with feelings of overload.

2. "Your bits are your responsibility": no tool or company can do this for you; you have to manage your own e-mail.

3. "To achieve bit literacy, let the bits go": keep the inbox empty.

It's not enough to get the inbox *nearly* empty, like down to a few dozen messages when it has held several hundred for the past few months. This means getting the count to zero—exactly zero—at least once a day. (Of course, this excludes days the user isn't on e-mail, like weekends and holidays.)

Although it takes a small amount of discipline, it's actually not difficult or time-consuming to maintain an empty inbox. Removing e-mails from the inbox doesn't mean doing all the work described in them; it just means moving them to the right place, like a todo list, so that you can work on them once the inbox is empty. For example, an e-mail may arrive announcing a new long-term project. Completing the work that the e-mail *refers to* may take months, but managing the e-mail message *itself* only takes a

---

* There are exceptions, of course. For example, users can—and should—unsubscribe from newsletters that they don't need. And in a team or office environment, bit literacy training can teach people how to reduce the amount of irrelevant e-mail they send to coworkers.

second or two. If you can distinguish between an e-mail and the thing it refers to, you'll be well on your way toward bit literacy.

Each daily emptying can be accomplished in the three easy steps described below. As the "steady-state" method, it assumes the inbox was emptied yesterday; the inbox should only contain e-mails that came in since yesterday (or the most recent zero count).* Users who are new to the method will, of course, need to first go through the step of emptying the inbox for the very first time. That process, called "induction," is described later in the chapter.

The daily "steady-state" method

Let's assume that you come into work in the morning, sit down at the computer, and see a new batch of e-mail. Perhaps there are twenty, fifty, or even a hundred new messages. Whatever the incoming volume of messages, don't worry; the e-mail inbox was empty yesterday, and you can empty it again today. All it takes is this three-step process:

Step 1: Read all personal e-mails, then delete them.

Step 2: Delete all spam mail.

Step 3: Engage FYIs and action items, then delete them. In particular:

 – Delete or file all FYIs, optionally reading them first.

 – Finish all quick "two-minute" todos, then delete them.

 – Move all big todos to a bit-literate todo list, then delete them.

Each step is covered in detail below.

---

* If you maintain multiple e-mail accounts, you should empty *each* of them daily—a good reason to keep e-mail accounts to a minimum.

Step 1: Personal e-mail

First look for the most *relevant* messages: e-mail from family and friends. Open each message and read it. Savor it. Do whatever you want: save it elsewhere on the computer, perhaps in a "scrapbook" folder, print it out to post on the refrigerator at home, or forward it to a friend. Take this time to write a reply, if you want. But when you're done with each personal e-mail, delete it. Nothing, no matter how important, is allowed to stay in the inbox.

Admittedly, this policy might sound unusual in some offices. Personal e-mail comes *first*? Yes, it should, and that's our policy at my consulting firm. We encourage employees to engage their personal e-mail before anything else. The alternative is distasteful—that personal e-mail should wait until *all* other e-mails are handled, thereby demoting one's personal relationships below the importance of an interoffice memo. (Of course, this step won't be relevant to people working at companies that prohibit personal e-mail.)

Bit literacy is a discipline that enables people to work more effectively in the bit world, so as to live more fully outside of it. For practicing the discipline, users deserve this payoff when they check e-mail. Personal messages should come first.

Step 2: Spam

Now that the most relevant e-mail is out of the inbox, find and delete the most *irrelevant* messages: spam. Bit-literate users must have a strategy for managing spam, either with mail filters or a "white list" service, to delete spam before it ever gets to the inbox.* Still, a few spam messages may get through the filters. Seek those out—they're usually easy to spot by their Subject lines—and delete them. Now the inbox is free from the most irrelevant messages.

---

* I use a "white list" service called SpamArrest, but there are many spam-fighting tools to choose from.

With the first two steps completed, we have now cleared the inbox of the most relevant, and the most irrelevant, messages. The remaining e-mails aren't as personally meaningful as a note from a family member, but they now require your full attention. In fact, this third step represents the core of the e-mail method. Lots of people know how to read e-mails from their spouse and delete spam messages; not many people know how to handle the work-related messages that overload them every day. The speed and ease with which you can move through the third step may largely determine how well you perform in your job. This is the real test of e-mail management.

Step 3: Engaging FYIs and action items

First, make sure that the inbox messages are sorted by date, with the oldest message on the top of the list. You'll deal with the oldest message first, and work your way down to the most recent.

Now open each message, from top to bottom of the inbox, engage it as described below, and then file it or delete it from the inbox. Open, engage, move it out; open, engage, move it out; all the way through the inbox. When this step is done, the inbox will be empty.

How to engage a message depends on what type it is. Spam messages and personal mails are already gone from the inbox, and so there are only three types of e-mails left: newsletters, FYIs, and todos. As you march through the inbox, message by message, engage each e-mail as described below, depending on its type.

— *Newsletters:* Read each newsletter quickly, depending on how much time is available, then delete it. If you have very little time and many other e-mails to engage, then quickly scan the headlines and delete it. If you have more time, read more of the newsletter, and feel free to save any part of it that you may need to reference later. But then delete it. Whatever you do, don't save the newsletter to read later, since when the next issue arrives you'll then have *two* issues awaiting your attention. The less you have to read in order to stay informed, the better. (Managing newsletter subscriptions and saving clippings are covered in the media diet chapter.)

- *FYIs:* These are non-actionable messages that are just "for your information": an answer to a question or a meeting announcement, for example. Meeting announcements may need to be noted on a calendar, and some messages might have to be filed in a project folder for documentation, but most FYIs just need a quick scan.* In many FYIs your address may appear on the CC line, indicating that this may be optional reading. (Advanced users might prefer to set up filters to automatically send CCs to a separate folder, in order to scan and delete those messages once a day.) Whatever the FYI is, read it if necessary, then delete it or file it; but get it out of the inbox.

- *Todos:* Use the "two-minute rule" for todos: if it takes two minutes or less to complete, do it immediately, even if it means physically getting up from your chair and temporarily leaving the bit world. Once it's complete, delete the e-mail. On the other hand, if the todo requires more than two minutes of your time, forward it to your todo list—which must exist separate from the inbox—and then delete it. (See the next chapter for managing todos.)

In each case above, note the common fate of the e-mail: it must leave the inbox. Delete it, or file it elsewhere, but never allow an e-mail to remain in the inbox. The inbox is only a temporary holding place for incoming e-mail—for no longer than twenty-four hours—and never for long-term storage.

Following the method described above actually doesn't take much time—probably less time, in fact, than it took to read the chapter to this point. With practice, an inbox cleanout should take no more than a few minutes. The key is to apply it consistently, like

---

* You can also send an FYI to yourself by CC'ing or BCC'ing yourself when you e-mail someone else. This is a good way to document an e-mail you've sent.

flossing daily, so that it becomes second nature. E-mail overload, that chronic source of stress, is thus almost a trivial problem to solve. Cleaning the inbox doesn't mean doing all the work described in the messages; it just means moving the messages to their proper places. Only then, with an empty inbox, can you focus on the actual work to be done.

Induction

Before getting to the steady-state method, many users need to first go through induction, the one-time removal of long-standing overload. Induction takes an inbox full of e-mail from the past several days, weeks, months, or years, and gets the message count to zero—not near it, but *exactly* zero—in one massive cleanout. It's useful not just for first-timers in bit literacy, but also for experienced users at moments when the inbox is unnaturally full of messages—when returning from a long vacation, for example.

Although it may be intimidating to users with months or years of old messages sitting in the inbox, induction is the only solution that gets users on track for daily emptying. A more gradual approach may seem more attractive—"I'll just clean it out a little bit each day, and soon it will be empty"—but it probably won't succeed. Pledges of gradual reform, however earnest, won't work for users who have grown accustomed to a high message count. They need to see a zero count.

The good news is that induction is well within the reach of any user. Like the steady-state method, induction doesn't ask users to do all the work in the inbox; it only asks that they move the messages to where they belong—the todo list, calendar, and so on. An inbox with hundreds of messages can be cleaned out in this way in an hour or two of focused work. Thereafter, the inbox can be cleaned out daily in a few minutes.

The three steps in induction are similar to the steady-state method. Steps 1 and 2 are the same as above: read and delete all personal e-mails, and then delete all the spam.

Step 3 of induction starts by deleting newsletters and FYIs in bulk:

— Sort the inbox by Subject and look for newsletters with several issues. These will appear together in the sorted inbox. Delete them all immediately, without reading them; this is no time to slow down and read what happened days, weeks, or months ago. If you're tempted to start opening them now, remind yourself that you survived this long without reading them. Delete them all and move on.

— To find FYIs and CCs, sort by From and Subject to see if there are any messages that you can delete without opening. Is there an announcement of a meeting that you already attended? Delete it. Is there a long series of e-mails on the same conversation thread that you can ignore? Delete them all.

Now sort by date, with the oldest message on top, and start opening the messages in order, one by one, to engage each. At this point the process is the same as the steady-state method, except with extreme bias toward speed. Be merciless in marching through these e-mails as quickly as possible—there's a long way to go before you reach the goal of zero count. Thus:

— If the message is an FYI, scan it, and file it if necessary, but delete it as quickly as you can, so you can move on to the next message.

— Use the two-minute rule and complete any quick todos right now. Don't put these off, even in a long induction process. Depending on how big the inbox is, you might have an hour or more of work on this step, but it's worth it to take care of these, finally, on your way to an empty inbox.

– Bigger action items are easy to handle: just move them to your todo list and move on. Don't even think of taking on a large todo right now; your goal is to clear these from the inbox and continue your march. You can take stock of your todo list once the inbox is empty.

Although it could take hours, induction will clear every message from a bulging inbox, no matter how big. The inbox will then be ready for a much easier daily cleanout, and users can apply the steady-state method daily, or more than once a day, depending on their preference. They can also choose how often to check e-mail.

How often to check, how often to empty

Some users prefer to check for new e-mail only once or twice a day. This minimizes the chance of distraction until the user is ready to engage the new messages. Other users prefer to keep their e-mail program constantly checking for e-mail throughout the day. This allows users to engage new e-mails as they appear, so that the inbox count never gets too high.

Bit-literate users should choose whichever method feels right. Different moments may also call for different choices. I usually have my e-mail program doing constant checks, but occasionally when I need to focus on a block of work, I'll temporarily halt the checks. In no case, though, should users (or companies) make a policy of artificially limiting anyone's access to incoming e-mail. Bit literacy gives users the freedom to choose when, and how often, to engage the bits.

Similarly, users have two choices for how often to clear the inbox: as e-mails arrive, or once or twice a day. Some users may opt to empty the inbox at the same time each day. In this case, the end of the day is a good time to do it, since that allows users to enjoy the evening and come in the next morning to see, perhaps, just a few new messages in the inbox. Users should make their own choice, as long as they never let the inbox go more than a day without emptying.

Users who are in an all-day meeting, or on a business trip, may find it difficult to empty the inbox at *any* time during the day. There is no easy solution for this; managing the inbox requires especially hard work when time is short. But there is no other choice. Since messages never stop coming in, the user must constantly stay in the pursuit of an empty inbox. The only alternatives are to let the inbox grow and grow, causing all the problems discussed earlier, or to hold the inbox steady at a certain count.

No halfway solutions

The "steady count" approach is a deceptively attractive halfway solution. Some users prefer to keep their inboxes at a modest count—five or ten messages—figuring that it's "close enough" to an empty inbox. People who do this often tell me that they're using their inbox as a todo list. Because they've let *most* of the bits go, they're not distracted by lots of messages; the few left in the inbox are their todos for the day. There are two problems with this approach, though:

– It's not their only todo list. Incoming e-mails are only one source of action items, so these users always maintain some other list— in a notebook, or in a separate todo list program—and as a result they can't see all their todos in one place. They have to spend time switching from list to list, which drains productivity and makes prioritization difficult. Using a single bit-literate todo list, as described in the next chapter, solves this problem *and* keeps the inbox empty.

– By keeping a steady count, the user never gets the "done" feeling of seeing an empty inbox. In fact, the user is doing the same amount of work as he would to hold the inbox at a constant count of zero; he's just not reaping the benefit.

The worst halfway solution is to delete some e-mail, but not all of it, day after day. When an especially busy day results in an unusually high message count, it's tempting to delete most of the messages, like spam and FYIs, but allow the todos to sit in the inbox. The next day brings in a new batch of e-mail, sitting on yesterday's action items. Now it's easier to go through the new mail than dive back into yesterday's stale batch, and the user may then let some of the new todos sit in the inbox with yesterday's.

After a few days of this, you can guess what the inbox looks like: e-mail overload with an infernal twist. The inbox is bulging with a pure, high-octane feed of big action items. It's worse than a garden-variety inbox, which at least has a few messages that are easily deleted. Now the user is overloaded only with urgent items, and new messages are still pouring in. It's now much harder to catch up to the empty inbox. Letting e-mails sit in the inbox for more than a day can be a dangerous slippery slope.

There is only one sustainable solution to e-mail overload, and that's to achieve emptiness every day. It's such a simple solution that it may seem attractive to apply it only temporarily or partially—but don't be fooled. The method is an all-or-nothing proposition: either the message count gets to zero once a day, or there's a problem.

Reactions to zero

An empty inbox means a count of zero—exactly zero—e-mails. There's a categorical difference between the experience of having "a few e-mails" and none at all. People who have worked for years with a bulging inbox and see the zero message count for the first time can have some pretty strong reactions, like this e-mail someone sent me shortly after adopting the method:

How does it feel?

> Strange: it's never been like that before, so it takes some
> getting used to.

Freeing: I open Outlook and sometimes there's this big
white space. With nothing to distract me I can focus on the
things I want to focus on.

Efficient: I certainly feel as though I can respond to email
more efficiently. Again, with nothing to distract me from
new e-mail, I can focus on responding to that mail more
effectively.

Strange, freeing, and efficient: that's an excellent way to describe
bit literacy. But some users have a harder time when they first
encounter an empty inbox. As one user wrote me, on seeing a zero
count for the first time:

It's 100% empty right now. It feels weird. empty. A VOID.
Like my e-mail crashed or something.
No reading pane, no nothing! Withdrawals!

Another user wrote perhaps the single most accurate reason I've
ever read for why most users don't take up this discipline:

To tell you the truth, it's freeing but scary to have an
empty e-mail box. I've spent a lot of my days scrolling back
and forth through all my e-mails and feeling the urgency.
Now I have to focus on real projects.

And that is exactly the point of the method. The sooner the inbox
is empty, the sooner the user can get to productive work.

Other challenges

For some users, the issue isn't the inbox but "the inboxes." Many people own multiple e-mail accounts, each accumulating its own e-mail bitstream and racking up its own message count. The obvious way to remove the load, in this case, is to minimize the number of e-mail accounts—simplifying, for example, to one for work and one for personal use.* Any other superfluous accounts should be shut down. (Just e-mail your friends and coworkers not to e-mail you there any more, and contact the e-mail host to close the account. It's a free and painless process, and it lets go of one more bitstream.)

Another challenge is practicing bit literacy in a team environment. Some individual team members with a zero count may be enduring needless e-mail volume from teammates, a problem that could be solved with better training or team e-mail policies. For example, guidelines can be set for who should get CC'd on various messages, or when to use the phone instead of e-mail. The most important part of the solution is for each individual on the team to keep their own inbox clean.

About instant messaging

Some users (and teams) supplement their e-mail usage with instant messaging, or chat. IM offers more immediacy than e-mail, displaying each line of text as the sender finishes typing it. This can be invaluable in situations where real-time communication is important—many online stores, for example, offer a feature to chat with customer service. On a project team, IM can grant an easy way for teammates to communicate quickly, especially if

* In addition to a work account and a personal account, some bit-literate users also maintain a "junk account" to use when registering for websites, so that it can accumulate any spam mail that comes in as a result. Of course, this doesn't need to be emptied daily.

they're in remote offices. Of course, phone calls also offer real-time communication, but it's often quicker and easier to dash off a brief note in the IM program.

The main disadvantage of IM is that it offers one more incoming bitstream to manage, in addition to the e-mail inbox. Instant messages can be just as distracting as new e-mails—if not more so, since IM's immediacy creates the expectation of immediate response. E-mails can sit comfortably for a few hours without a response, but people want their IMs answered immediately.

If invited to use IM, bit-literate users should think carefully about whether it's worth opening a new bitstream. Some jobs may require IM, and some users may enjoy having another way to connect with friends online. But many users will find that e-mail is sufficient. It's best to avoid two bitstreams when one will do.

Clearing the Sent Items folder

A final note on e-mail overload: for many users, the inbox isn't the only source of stress. Many people maintain a Sent Items folder holding hundreds or thousands of messages they've sent in the past. This isn't as immediate a problem as the inbox, since users aren't expected to review or respond to their sent messages. But the bits are always present, always growing, and they weigh on the user. (A large Sent Items folder can contribute to an e-mail crash, too, just like an inbox.)

Some users occasionally work on manually cleaning out their Sent Items—deleting sent e-mails they don't want saved on the computer, or deleting especially old or irrelevant messages. This is a needlessly time consuming task. Others maintain the Sent Items folder to function as a separate filing system—a use it was never intended for. Instead, whenever users send a message that they want to save, they should BCC themselves so that it comes back through the inbox, allowing them to engage it in the inbox, along with all other incoming e-mails. Users can then file the message in the right place—a dedicated project folder, for example. (The proper use of the file system is discussed in a later chapter.)

Meanwhile, users should assign the e-mail program the task of keeping the Sent Items folder clean, by setting a "time window." If the e-mail program contains this feature, the user should set it to delete all sent items after a certain period, like a week. That way the user can retrieve recently sent items, but there is never more than a week of e-mail saved. By letting the bits go in this way, the user is free from an unnecessary task and can get on with more important things.

Chapter 5: **Managing Todos**

Users with an empty inbox need to know what to do next, and that requires proper todo management. In fact, managing todos may be considered even more important than managing e-mail, since this is where users begin to really do their job. Bit literacy is essential: it minimizes the time it takes to organize todos, in order to maximize the amount of time for working on them.

The challenge is overload. Just as with incoming e-mail, each day can bring a barrage of new todos, adding to yesterday's. But e-mail management alone can't address this problem. While many todos arrive in the inbox, not all do. The boss might assign a new task during a meeting, or you might agree to a new task during a phone call. Even writing an e-mail can do it: if you send someone *else* a todo, you've also essentially assigned yourself a todo of making sure that they complete the task.

Todos differ from e-mail in one main respect: they actually need to get done. The e-mail inbox collects bits that just need to be read, and then deleted or moved to the right place. Todos are the work itself. Overload is distracting and irritating in e-mail, but it is a serious problem on a todo list. It takes real focus, sometimes sustained over a period of time, to complete some todos; managing *many* todos requires prioritizing them, in order to focus on the right thing at every moment. Anything less can threaten one's job, or career.

Users need a robust tool, then, to manage todos: something outside the e-mail program that prioritizes todos in a bit-literate way—letting the bits go—and protects the user from undue stress. And it has to be a single tool, so that users can find all their todos in one place. Users can't prioritize or focus very well if they're maintaining multiple lists. It's a tall order for one tool. So what do most users choose?

Paper. Usually many pieces of paper. Often painfully many. Small, fluorescent squares crowding the sides of computer monitors, cluttering whole workspaces; scribbled receipts and cocktail napkins, stuffed into pockets, posted on refrigerator doors, thrown into piles. Notebooks filled with scrawl, file folders with little colored tabs, printouts of reminders and instructions. Paper. Reams of it, decks of it, stacks of it, cluttering our eye-level view and scattered about underfoot; paper, filling up our lives, distracting our senses, getting in the way, and awaiting, someday, a laborious cleanout and final shredding. In anything but small amounts, using paper for todos is a plague on productivity. It is not the tool for the job.

Today's information overload is caused by bits, and so the tool to manage the overload must work with bits. Using paper to manage todos simply does not make sense. A long time ago it was the best choice, but today it's slow, unnecessarily painful, and more than a little ridiculous. You might as well do all your business travel on horseback.

This doesn't stop some people from trying out paper-based solutions. Some companies today sell methods that promise to get people organized with a complex array of notebooks, folders, and other paper-based tools—all sold, of course, by those same companies. Beyond the obvious flaw of being based in paper, the sheer complexity of these methods is both a selling point (it looks more powerful that way) and a barrier to anyone who actually wants to get things done. The more flowcharts and frameworks in the method, the more time it takes to learn and practice, and the less *productive* the user becomes. Complex paper-based methods are great for selling seminars and associated materials; they're just not good at making people productive. What people need today is a simple, elegant bit-based method that allows them to get to work as quickly as possible: bit literacy.

Still, most people today use paper to manage their todos—not as part of any special paper-based method or system, but because paper is what they have on hand. They've never learned anything different, and besides, little fluorescent paper squares are sort of fun to look at. The problem is that these notes, if used in any significant number, cause clutter. The scene is so familiar that it's almost a cliché: the computer monitor ringed with sticky notes, overlapping and competing for the user's attention. The mess is symptomatic of the user's underlying lack of bit literacy. It's as though the bits, running wild inside the computer, have spilled out onto the monitor in paper form.

Paper is invaluable for jotting down the occasional note, but it's not good for managing todos. Thus bit literacy calls for the user to minimize their use of paper and use a bit-based system to manage their todos. To explain the bit-literate method, we must first examine why, exactly, paper is so ineffective.

There are two reasons why bit-literate users must not rely on paper to manage their todos: scale and time.

Paper and scale

Scale is always a problem when we try to apply paper solutions to bit-based problems. Paper notes are effective only in small numbers: one sticky note works fine, standing out politely, but a few more start to become distracting. A couple dozen sticky notes are a mess, barely fitting onto the monitor where we can see them all. And more than that are impossible to manage physically, let alone mentally.

But "more than that" is exactly what the bit world brings. Bits are infinite. In order to thrive in the digital age, we need a solution that scales up to handle *any* number of todos. Paper can't scale, since it's physically constrained by the space it occupies and our ability to see it. If someone really wanted to use sticky notes to manage their digital todos, they would have to find a place to display hundreds, if not thousands, of them.* Paper—even in an obsessively organized notebook—is no substitute for managing bits correctly in the first place. Only bits can scale in quantity.

Paper also doesn't scale in the amount of data it can hold, again because of physical constraints. A todo can come with an arbitrary amount of information attached, and it's impossible to rely on paper to contain it all. For example, consider the todo of answering some questions based on several pages of meeting notes. No paper-based method—not sticky notes, not a handwritten notebook—could easily store that todo, let alone a bitstream of many such todos arriving every day. Bits, though, scale perfectly to hold any amount of data in a small container. A good example of this is the e-mail inbox, which can contain a long e-mail while only displaying a Subject line of a few words. (As shown below, a bit-literate todo list offers a similar feature.) But paper can't scale; the more data it carries, the more physical space it occupies.

Paper and time

The drawback of scale is secondary to an even bigger flaw. Paper is totally unable to match bits in the most important aspect of managing todos: time. Todo management, after all, is the process of managing our attention over time. When a user faces dozens of items on a todo list, the challenge isn't to finish everything all at once, but rather to decide which todos are important to work on now versus later, and in what order. When todos are abundant, time is the scarce resource that needs to be managed.

---

* Sticky Notes, a popular software program a few years back, allowed users to plaster the entire screen with virtual slips of paper, as though the edges of the physical monitor just weren't big enough. The virtual notes had all the drawbacks of real paper—clutter, distraction, lack of scale—and almost none of the advantages of bits.

There is no todo management without time management. Every todo has a time when it needs attention, and for many todos that time is in the future—and not until then. That's why we often need to create a todo *today* for something that needs to be done in the *future*.

For example, when I drop off the dry cleaning on Tuesday, the cleaner tells me that the clothes will be ready for pickup on Friday. Since I'm most aware of the todo when I drop off the clothes, I should create the todo that day—Tuesday—even though the todo isn't yet active. The question then becomes *how* to create the todo. One possibility is to write a sticky note and put it on the refrigerator—"pick up dry cleaning Friday"—but then I have to look at that todo for three days without being able to work on it. It's a poor solution: either I'm needlessly distracted by the todo for several days, or I manage to ignore it, thereby rendering it useless as a reminder.

Now consider what happens when the todo doesn't become active for a longer period—a week, or a month, or a year. For example, if the phone company overcharged your account and you want to make sure the error was corrected, you'll have to check next month's statement. In this case, a sticky note would be really annoying. You don't want to be reminded every day for several weeks to check the statement next month; it's a needless distraction, and you may train yourself to ignore it by the time it becomes relevant. Instead, you should only *begin* to be reminded at that later date. A paper calendar might handle a few such reminders, but only in small quantity and with little or no accompanying data.

Now take the two examples above—the dry cleaning and the phone bill—and multiply them by a thousand. That's the scale of todos in the bit world, and no paper solution can come close to addressing it. Bit literacy allows users to manage any number of todos across arbitrarily long periods of time.

The todo's life cycle

Managing todos properly requires an understanding of how they work. The four phases in the life of a todo are creation, inactivity, activation, and completion:

– *Creation* is, obviously, the moment at which the user creates the todo. The user should create the todo right away, as soon as he learns of the need for it, even if the todo doesn't require action until later.

– *Inactivity* is a possible period of "hibernation" between creation and activation. Some todos need action right when they're created, and so they skip this step; other todos, like the dry cleaning example, may be inactive for days or longer before they "wake up." Inactive todos must remain out of sight, where they won't distract or overload the user, until they activate.

– *Activation* is the moment at which the todo is available to be completed, and when it begins to remind the user about its existence. The todo then remains active until it's complete. (That is, unless the user makes the todo inactive again for some amount of time. This involves redating a todo into the future, which is covered below.) For example, the dry cleaning todo activates on Friday, when the clothes are available to be picked up.

– *Completion* is when the todo is done, and checked off the todo list. It could also mean the user deleting a todo, if it has become irrelevant since its creation.

For a todo list to be an appropriate choice for bit-literate users, it must allow todos to move through each phase above. (Most todo lists, as we'll see later, miss the second phase—inactivity—which leads to all sorts of problems.) It also must have a simple interface, allowing quick and easy usage. And as described previously, a todo list must be based in bits—not paper—in order to meet the challenges of scale and time. With those requirements in mind, we can state the four components of a bit-literate todo list:

1. Each todo is associated with a particular day.

2. Users can create new todos via e-mail, either for today or a day in the future.

3. Each todo has a priority ranking within its day.

4. Each todo can contain a detail field as well as a summary, much the same way an e-mail can contain a message body as well as a Subject line.

Surprisingly few tools today contain these components—not because any of the features are complex or expensive to create, but because the technology industry is mostly unaware of bit literacy. Even so, bit-literate users must use a todo list with *all* four aspects listed above: association with date, compatibility with e-mail, ranking within a day, and a detail field. A todo list program without all four components is like a trampoline intended to get people to the moon. It's a cute idea, and it may even be fun to try out, but it's not going to work.

Flawed solutions are common. Paper-based systems, as described above, are by definition incapable of being bit-literate. Software and Web-based tools are mostly ineffective, too, exhibiting one of two problems:

– *Some are too simple:* These todo lists offer attractive, simple interfaces that allow users to easily add todos to a list. But the features stop there. They can't associate todos with a day, and strangely enough, some don't even offer a detail field for todos—only a summary. It's as if an e-mail program used Subject lines only, but no message bodies. Regardless of any other aspects of a todo list, the absence of a detail field limits it to being a kind of online collection of sticky notes—good for quick reminders and grocery-shopping lists, but not much else.

The failure to associate todos with days makes these services even less effective.

— *Others are too complex:* In contrast to the simplistic todo list, this approach is to pack every possible feature into a single product. By trying to be "everything to everyone," the tool ends up being not much for anyone. With a high-tech mess of menus, tabs, colors, windows, wizards, flags, panes, and popups, even simple tasks are a challenge. Microsoft Outlook is a prime example of this approach.* Such tools overload users with too much irrelevant information, which makes them less productive. The more users have to filter out—whether inactive todos or irrelevant interface features—the less time and energy they have left to get their work done. A bit-literate todo list must be simple enough to keep the user focused on their work—not the tool itself.

The bit-literate todo list: Gootodo

The four components of a bit-literate todo list are examined below. Each is illustrated by an example from Gootodo, a Web-based todo list I developed some time ago, available at Gootodo.com. (The name is short for "Good Experience todo list.") Someday, when bit literacy is better known, there will be many todo lists that offer these features, but for now the discussion must be restricted to Gootodo, since it's the only todo list that includes all four components and a simple interface.

1. Each todo is associated with a particular day.

A todo list should distinguish between active todos (those we have to work on today) and inactive todos (those we can ignore today because they become relevant in the future). The todo list should

---

* As of February 2007 the official Outlook help page on Microsoft's website lists a *fourteen-step* process for creating a todo from an e-mail: http://office.microsoft.com/en-us/outlook/HA012293021033.aspx

focus users on today's todos *only;* those waiting in the future should stay there and not be distractions. Therefore, Gootodo includes a calendar that allows different todos to sit on different days. Today's todos are thus kept separate from inactive todos, which are stored on their future activation dates.

A calendar may seem like a small addition, but it's essential in allowing users to "let the bits go" by ignoring future todos, so as to focus only on what they need to work on now. When a user logs in to Gootodo, he sees a list of today's todos *only.* There is no other indication of future todos, just a calendar that shows the current month and day. If the user wants to explore future days, he can click a future day in the calendar, and that day's list will appear. But that requires active effort by the user; by default, Gootodo focuses the user only on what he needs to get done today.

Shown below is today's list, assuming today is January 9, and it contains only one item. There may be many other todos waiting on future days, but they're not displayed here. The user would have to click a future day in the calendar, on the right side of the page, to see them; otherwise, irrelevant todos remain hidden from view.

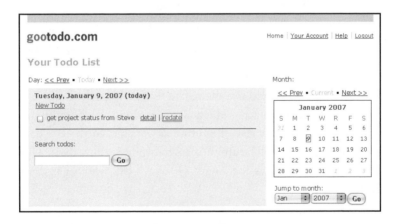

In addition to being assigned to a day, every todo is accompanied by a "redate" link. Clicking this, a user can send the todo into the future—to tomorrow's list, or next week, or any time in the next year. This makes the todo inactive and resets the activation date into the future. It also removes the todo from today's list. Conversely, a user can activate an inactive link by redating a future todo back to today. This gives the user full control of time: he can send today's todos into the future, and he can send future todos back to today. (Past days can only hold completed todos.)

Clicking the "redate" link in the example above brings up a popup calendar:

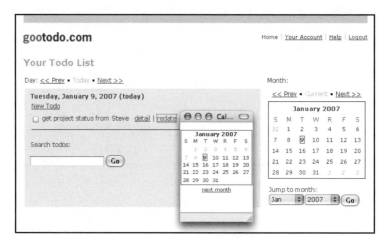

Clicking a future date in the popup sends the todo to that day and removes it from today's list.

Bit-literate users should use the redate feature liberally, because it helps them procrastinate—which is a *good* thing. It's often useful to move a todo as far into the future as possible, to the last date on which it would still be appropriate to begin working on it. This "letting go" minimizes the length of today's list, which has three major benefits:

— Users are less distracted and can focus only on what they need to get done today.

— Users set themselves up for success; the shorter the todo list, the greater chance they'll finish it.

– Once all of today's todos are complete, users can feel a sense of relief knowing they're *done*.

Of course, if users finish everything on today's list with time to spare, they can look at future days and begin completing those todos as well. (In practice, that rarely happens; it's enough just to try to get today's work done.) If today's list *isn't* all done, then at midnight, the undone todos roll over to tomorrow's list.

2. Users can create new todos via e-mail, either for today or a day in the future.

Like the calendar, this is a feature that is at once massively important, not particularly hard to create, and practically unknown in other todo lists. Gootodo offers the ability to create dated todos from e-mail.

E-mail is a natural choice for creating todos because we can use it in so many different places and contexts, on a variety of different devices—much like the diversity of times, places, and contexts in which we create new todos. For example, if you're in a meeting, with access to no device except a BlackBerry, and you think of a new todo, you can simply e-mail the todo in to your list. From work, home, the airport, or a streetside Internet cafe, anywhere you have e-mail access, you have the ability to add items to your todo list—for today or any future day.

This feature is important for the e-mail management method described in the previous chapter. Remember Step 3, when you have to move big todos from the inbox to the todo list? It's as easy as clicking the Forward button. Many todos arrive via e-mail, after all, so it makes sense to allow e-mail to tie in to the todo list.

When it receives an e-mail, Gootodo creates a new todo as such:

– the Subject line of the e-mail becomes the summary, or title, of the todo

– the body of the e-mail becomes the detail, or body, of the todo

– the To: address determines the activation date

For example, you could send this e-mail to create a todo on today's list:

```
From: reader@example.com
To: today@gootodo.com
Subject: file expense report


Remember to include receipts for rental car and snacks.
```

The available e-mail addresses are easy to remember. Send the e-mail to today@gootodo.com and the todo shows up on today's list. Or send it to tomorrow@gootodo.com and the todo will *not* show up on today's list. Instead it will be completely hidden until tomorrow, unless you actively click forward in the calendar to see tomorrow's todo list.

There are many other available e-mail addresses. The seven day names—monday@gootodo.com, tuesday@gootodo.com, and so on—send the todo to the appropriate day in the next seven days. Time durations work, too: 2d@gootodo.com sends the todo out two days, 1w@gootodo.com sends it out one week, and 6m@gootodo.com sends it out six months. The "d", "w", and "m" addresses can use any number from 1 to 12 (and the address is forgiving—the number can appear before or after the letter and it will work). You can be even more efficient by setting up nicknames in your e-mail program for the most commonly used addresses. Addressing an e-mail to "3d" would then send the e-mail to 3d@gootodo.com, saving you the hassle of typing out the entire address.

Finally, specific dates in the calendar all have their own e-mail addresses. Send the e-mail to dec1 or 1dec and the e-mail will appear on December 1. All 365 days in the calendar work, with common variations in the dates accepted. 18march, march18th, 18mar, and mar18@gootodo.com all go to March 18.

These addresses make it easy to let the bits go. You can send a todo to your future self and then stop worrying about it in the present, so that you can focus on today's work only. This is especially significant because it reduces an infinity of bits to a finite amount that's manageable within the time available. This method finally solves the problems of e-mail and todo overload.

A bit-literate todo list also gives users one other benefit: they become better at followup, a surprisingly big benefit covered in detail later in the chapter.

3. Each todo has a priority ranking within its day.

As described above, the calendar allows users to prioritize by date: relevant todos today, and irrelevant todos in the future. Given the importance of prioritization, it only makes sense that Gootodo also allows users to sort the priority of todos *within* a given day. (This is not unique to Gootodo, but it's an essential aspect of a bit-literate todo list.) Each todo is accompanied by a series of up and down arrows which move the todo up or down the list, either by one todo or all the way to the top or bottom.

A good exercise to begin each day is to review and prioritize today's todos: redate non-critical todos into future days, and then sort to-day's todos, top to bottom, from most to least important. You then have an ordered list of everything you need to get done today, and you always know what you should be working on at any moment: the todo on the top of the list.

Figure 1

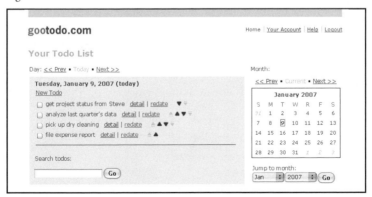

For example, the todo list may look like Figure 1 (previous page).

If the user decides that the expense report—now at the bottom of the list—is most important, he can change the priority of the todo. There are two up-arrows to the right of the todo: an underlined arrow that takes the todo to the very top of the list, and another arrow that takes the todo up by one spot. Clicking the underlined arrow results in this todo list:

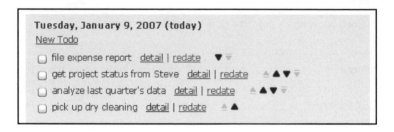

The todos are now in the right order. Throughout the day the user can work through them, from top to bottom, always knowing the one thing he should focus on. Assuming the inbox is also empty, once all four todos are checked complete, the user will be *done*. This is what the empty todo list will look like:

Tuesday, January 9, 2007 (today)
New Todo

- ✔ pick up dry cleaning   detail | redate
- ✔ analyze last quarter's data   detail | redate
- ✔ get project status from Steve   detail | redate
- ✔ file expense report   detail | redate

The user will have then achieved emptiness and can finish the day free from any overload—or even start working on the next day's todos.

4. Each todo can contain a detail field as well as a summary, much the same way an e-mail can contain a message body as well as a Subject line.

Each day's todo list—for today or a day in the future—shows the summaries, or titles, of all the todos that day. What the summary view does *not* show is the detail of the todos. The user must click a todo's "detail" link to see it. This way users can store arbitrary amounts of information inside their todos, but only see one-line titles on the summary view. It's an essential safeguard against clutter.

In the earlier example, clicking the "detail" link to the right of "file expense report" would bring up the detail view of the todo:

Todo details can contain any sort of text: call notes, e-mail threads, followup history, journal entries, and so on. For example, you can create a todo called "call John," and in the details, you can include the entire meeting agenda, John's different phone numbers, and the thread of recent e-mails that brought on the call. Everything necessary to complete the todo is in the details, but on the todo list it only says "call John." (The color of the "detail" link tells whether the todo contains something in the detail field. Purple means something is in the detail field; blue means it's empty.)

Using the detail field, users can also manage and track a large todo that encompasses many different steps. As each step is complete, the user can note it in the detail field, and then check the entire todo done when all the steps are complete.

Omitted features

The examples above show how Gootodo offers the four essential components of a bit-literate todo list with a simple user interface. There are some other optional features, too, accessible by clicking the "Your Account" link on the top of the page. In general, Gootodo was built to be as simple as possible to allow bit-literate work, but no simpler. This means that Gootodo can't be everything to everyone, and so it omits some possible features.

Such simplicity comes at a cost. To the techie user, a bit-literate todo list may come across as pedestrian, even dull. The response Gootodo gets from techies is often "Is this *it?*" along with a request for more, flashier, higher-tech features. There are good reasons why Gootodo omits most of these features.

The most common feature techies ask for is categorization: the ability to sort todos into types, like "home" and "work"; or high, medium, and low priority. Such features would require Gootodo to display todos in different colors, multiple hierarchies, or with accompanying "tags," or keywords. Other requests ask for sub-lists that track multiple steps within one todo—something that Gootodo users can already do easily enough with the detail field, as described above.*

Features like these might be useful in some cases, but if they don't support the central idea of bit literacy—letting the bits go—they shouldn't be in the tool. Categorization, rather than decreasing the user's load of bits, would actually add *more* bits that the user needs to manage. Moreover, such features invite users to play around

---

* Still other requested features include AJAX, RSS, and other faddish acronyms that are only understood by techies and the journalists who love them.

with the tool more than they need to. Productivity is measured in the amount of work users get done *outside* of the todo list, not the amount of time they spend organizing the list itself.

The truth is that many users just don't want to do their work. Given a choice between completing a todo or spending several minutes deciding what color it should be, lots of people—especially techies, who love playing with software—would choose the latter. Colors are fun, pretty, and don't require much thought. Doing the actual work in the todo requires time and energy, risks failure, and might not be any fun. Users are best served by a tool that encourages the discipline of actually getting the work done, rather than endlessly tweaking the system.

About the long list

A bit-literate todo list gets users back to work by focusing them only on what they need to do today. There's only one downside: if the user has too many todos, the todo list quickly exposes that uncomfortable truth. Once the user is done setting things up, the list of todos that need immediate attention may stretch far down the screen—a demoralizing sight. Some users, despairing, reflexively look for technology to save them: perhaps a different feature, or multiple todo lists, would help stem the tide. As one user put it in an e-mail:

> What should I do about very long gootodo lists (150 items
> and counting)? I'm a follower of [complex paper-based
> system] and have tried to think of this as my next actions
> list. Since you advocate 'going to zero' on e-mail and
> gootodo ... What's your recommendation on this? Should I
> create ANOTHER LIST as my 'don't forget' list? Or is it OK to
> carry long lists like this one in gootodo?

The plain fact is that having too much work isn't something that a todo list can fix. Todo lists can only show what there is to do, and help users organize and prioritize it all. If there's too much work to do, then a good todo list should at least make that clear, so users can think about how to re-organize or even turn down some of the work. The worst thing a todo list can do is obscure the problem, distracting users with a thick layer of needless features and complexity.

Users should, however, procrastinate when appropriate. If a user can't realistically get to all 150 items *today*, he should forward them to some point in the future when he can get to them. But if he sees that he can't *ever* complete all his work—if he thinks he may be carrying 150 todos forever—then that's an issue he must address separately from any software or system. Talking to the boss may get some of those action items re-assigned to someone else. But no system, no matter how complex or high-tech, can address such a problem that originates outside the bit world.

A good measure of success in todo management is the number of items sitting on today's list. Similar to the message count in e-mail, the todo count is a quick benchmark to see how close the user is to being "done." And just as bit-literate users should empty the e-mail inbox once a day, they should also try to empty the todo list at least once a week. (It's unrealistic to finish the todo list every single day, since some todos take several days to complete.) It's a great feeling to leave the office on a Friday afternoon, knowing that the weekend is starting and *both* the e-mail inbox and todo list are empty: you're *done*. (Until Monday, that is.)

Using Gootodo for followup

There's one more benefit of Gootodo that's worth exploring. It's easily overlooked, because it's not something that people expect from a todo list, but it's a monumentally important benefit to bit-literate users: followup. By using CC and BCC in e-mail, a user can turn Gootodo into the single best followup machine ever created.

The pipeline of followup looks like this:

- You send someone a question to answer or a todo to accomplish.

- They send you back a confirmation (acknowledging that they understand the question or accept the todo). If they don't confirm within a certain amount of time, you send followups until they do.

- They send you a completion (either answering the question or otherwise showing that the todo is done) or cancellation (declining the question or todo, presumably giving a reason, possibly directing you to ask someone else). If they don't complete or cancel within some amount of time, you send followups until they do.

There are two situations, then, that call for followup:

1. *Confirmation:* When you send someone a todo, you must follow up to make sure "they've got it," promising to deliver completion within a certain amount of time.

2. *Completion:* If someone doesn't complete in time, you must follow up to remind them what they promised and ask them when they'll complete—or if they're cancelling. (If the recipient still doesn't complete the todo after a certain amount of time, you can then take that as their cancellation.)

Diligently sending followups in these two situations ensures that there's no way to forget or "drop bits"; every single todo you send will eventually come to some resolution. Gootodo works in both cases, allowing you to follow up on confirmation and completion steps.

Example 1: Following up in a week

Here's an example of completion. Suppose you, at reader@example .com, ask your coworker Ben Smith to send you the PFR Report.

Date: April 9, 20..
From: reader@example.com
To: ben.smith@example.com
BCC: 1w@gootodo.com
Subject: please send me the PFR report

Ben - could you please send me the PFR report - never got
it from you. Thanks.
R.

Maybe Ben has been dragging his heels, hoping you'd forget all about the report. So when he sees this e-mail, he ignores it, hoping you'll get distracted by work and forget about this undone todo within a few days.

Wrong. You BCC'd 1w@gootodo.com, so it will appear on your todo list in one week. This way, if Ben hasn't replied within a week to give you confirmation or completion, you can follow up again. And at that point you can paste in the original e-mail.

Date: April 16, 20..
From: reader@example.com
To: ben.smith@example.com
BCC: 1w@gootodo.com
Subject: awaiting your reply - please send me the PFR
report

Ben - just following up from my note last week (see below).
Could you send the PFR report, please?

R.

> Date: April 9, 20..
> From: reader@example.com
> To: ben.smith@example.com
> Subject: please send me the PFR report
>
> Ben - could you please send me the PFR report—never got
it from you. Thanks.
> R.

Notice that you've *again* BCC'd 1w@gootodo.com, which creates another reminder for you a week from now. This way you can follow up again and again until Ben sends the report or at least acknowledges that he got your request.

Example 2: Following up in several months

This example demonstrates the month-day addressing feature. Let's start with the confirmation step, since this is where salespeople, and others who need followup, often get stuck. Some people acknowledge a todo with a "brush-off" response, postponing their reply to some time in the future.

Suppose you're trying to get a coworker, employee, or client to sign up for a monthly training session that she needs:

```
Date: September 5, 20..
From: reader@example.com
To: jane.williams@example.com
Subject: sign up for the Z1 training session?


Jane,

Are you ready to sign up for our monthly Z1 training
session? There are only a few slots left.

Thanks,
R.
```

Jane replies with a brush-off, figuring that you'll certainly forget about the todo within a few months:

```
Date: September 6, 20..
From: jane.williams@example.com
To: reader@example.com
Subject: Re: sign up for the Z1 training session?
```

R.—sure, just get back to me in early March and I'll be
ready to sign up.

Jane

Jane is mistaken. Gootodo allows you to send the todo to the
exact time of year she mentioned. Simply forward her e-mail to
march1@gootodo.com, as shown in the following:

Date: September 6, 20..
From: reader@example.com
To: march1@gootodo.com
Subject: Fwd: Re: sign up for the Z1 training session?

> Date: September 6, 20..
> From: jane.williams@example.com
> To: reader@example.com
> Subject: Re: sign up for the Z1 training session?
>
> R.—sure, just get back to me in early March and I'll be
ready to sign up.
>
> Jane

Having sent the e-mail, you can forget about the todo for several
months and focus on other work. Only when March 1 rolls around
will your todo list contain the todo, showing the following title:

> ☐ Fwd: Re: sign up for the Z1 Training session?

(Some users may prefer to rename the Subject line when they
forward the e-mail, so that the todo has a clearer title when the
todo pops up in March. A Subject like "Jane re Z1 training?"
might be a good one.)

Whatever the name of the todo, the detail field will contain the
body of the e-mail, reminding you what the todo is about. You
can paste the todo body in your followup note to Jane, and BCC

1w@gootodo.com to make sure you get a response to *this* followup. Best of all, you'll be sending the followup right on time:

```
Date: March 1, 20..
From: reader@example.com
To: jane.williams@example.com
BCC: 1w@gootodo.com
Subject: checking in—sign up for the Z1 training session?


Jane,
Just checking in on your e-mail from last September,
pasted below - you said you'd be ready to sign up for Z1
training in early March, and here we are! Are you ready to
sign up?


R.


> Date: September 6, 20..
> From: jane.williams@example.com
> To: reader@example.com
> Subject: Re: sign up for the Z1 training session?
>
> R.—sure, just get back to me in early March and I'll be
ready to sign up.
>
> Jane
```

Using Gootodo in this way, I've found that many people will respond immediately out of sheer amazement, shocked by my freakishly accurate timing. Weeks or months can pass by and I can get back to them, exactly on time, quoting their original note. This is to their delight or chagrin, depending on what I'm bringing up. More than one recipient has asked me if I'm psychic.

And that's the beauty of bit-literate todo management: by using bits to their advantage, I can have near-perfect accuracy and timeliness—even the appearance of psychic powers!—with *less* mental exertion than what other todo lists require. If I send a todo six months into the future, I can totally forget about the todo—letting the bits go—until it becomes relevant again and Gootodo brings it back to my attention.

There are many other ways Gootodo can be used for followup. Bit-literate users should explore Gootodo, or some other bit-literate todo list, and stay on the lookout for other ways to improve their effectiveness. Todo management, like all of bit literacy, is a lifelong discipline of continual improvement.

Chapter 6: **The Media Diet**

There's a saying at my alma mater: getting an education at MIT is like taking a drink from a firehose.* The same could be said for staying informed in the information-saturated environment we live in today. As Richard Saul Wurman put it in his 1989 book *Information Anxiety:* "One of the most anxiety-inducing side effects of the information era is the feeling that you have to know it all. Realizing your own limitations becomes essential to surviving an information avalanche; you cannot or should not absorb or even pay attention to everything." That book was published at a time before e-mail was popular, so the quote refers to the deluge of *print*-based information. The sentiment is even more relevant today. The age of bits has brought on a stupendous multiplication of information we're now invited to engage.

Consider the many kinds of media that vie for our attention today on a regular basis. These are just the periodical media, the sources that ask us to commit to reading, viewing, or listening on a regular basis. ("One-offs" like books and movies add even more to the noisy media environment.)

Offline media:

– Magazines
– Newspapers
– TV shows
– Radio programs

---

* For this reason I named my college comic strip "Firehose Tavern." The jokes were about that good.

Online:

- E-mail newsletters (one publisher writing to many readers)
- E-mail mailing lists (many readers contributing to one ongoing conversation)
- Websites, including blogs
- Newer types of online content: podcasts, "vlogs," "moblogs," and others

We have more media choice than any generation in history. Most reasonably well-off people living in urban or suburban areas have easy access to dozens of choices in each of the offline categories, and any user with an Internet connection has access to thousands or *millions* of choices in each of the online categories. The range of choices alone is staggering, without even trying to read, view, or listen to any of them. We might as well consider counting every grain of sand on the beach; just the scope of the issue is almost too big to grasp.

Such an overload of media can bring the same problems as a bulging inbox: it weighs on people, causing stress and anxiety. It may sound enticing to subscribe to the latest trade magazine or e-newsletter, but it's demoralizing to see a pile of issues awaiting reading—whether on the office desk or in the e-mail inbox. It cuts into productivity and generally decreases quality of life outside of work. (For that matter, seeing magazines and other media piling up at *home* can affect quality of life, too.)

The first step in achieving control over this media overload is not to feel guilty. You receive too much information, and it's not your fault. Just accept that there is more information than time, and that it's increasing every day. The free availability of bits ensures that whatever deluge exists today, there will be more tomorrow.

Just as with e-mail overload and todo overload, bit literacy offers a solution to media overload. Even though we have limited time for a limitless supply of media, bit literacy gives us the ability to survive, even thrive, in the deluge. We just have to learn the strategy and then be disciplined about practicing it. It does, however, require an active choice.

There are three possible ways to deal with too many media sources:

- Live by reaction: feel increasingly stressed and confused as more information sources appear and ask for more of your attention.

- Opt out: avoid the problem entirely by not reading or watching anything, digital or analog. (Ignorance is bliss.)

- Practice bit literacy: get *some* information—the *right* information—without trying to get all of it.

The bit-literate approach involves creating and maintaining a *media diet*, a constantly pruned set of publications (digital, print, and other media) that keeps us informed about what matters most to us, professionally and personally. Like every other part of bit literacy, this is a discipline that users must take responsibility for. No one else can create our media diet. If anything, the established media don't *want* us to have a media diet. We're more pliable as consumers and citizens if we live by reaction. Creating a media diet is thus somewhat subversive because it allows us to survive independently of what the publishers want us to do, which is to consume more media. But it's our only reasonable choice. In this environment of abundant information and scarce time, our job is to say "no"—early and often, more often than we might expect—and to say "yes" rarely, only when it suits our purposes. We still need the publishers, but we must engage them on our terms, not theirs.

A media diet isn't all that different, in fact, from the everyday diet of food and drink. Regardless of how serious you are about maintaining a healthy diet, it's essential to at least know that there *is* such a thing as a diet. Awareness is an essential first step toward health. And this is the problem that many technology users face:

they have never even heard of a media diet, let alone tried to create and live by one. Imagine if, ignorant of basic dietary practices, someone lived exclusively on hamburgers, french fries, donuts, and whatever else the fast food corporations sold; the person would experience serious health problems. The results of not following a media diet are similarly unhealthy. Living by reaction leads to stress; opting out leads to ignorance.

A healthy media diet, however, pays long-term dividends from a relatively tiny investment in time and discipline. Bit literacy allows you to create a media diet that...

— is based on what's important to you, not to any other person, publisher, or company;

— draws on the tiny minority of sources that do serve you some purpose;

— ignores the huge ocean of irrelevant or redundant sources;

— is an active portfolio that you can change, in order to keep it as pertinent as possible; and

— is as small as possible.

The last point, on minimizing size, deserves some focus. In creating your media diet you must draw on as few sources as possible, and spend as little time as possible, in order to be fully informed. Always remember that *time* is your most precious resource, so you must always look for ways to skip, scan, defer, prune, and delete sources from your media diet. "Let the bits go" in this context becomes "let the sources go." As with e-mail and todos, removing the overload leads to greater productivity and more peace of mind.

Once you have a media diet, you—and no one else—are in control of what you read, watch, and listen to. And you know the specific reasons *why* you engage each of your sources. Think of the media diet as a team of advisers you've hired to inform you about the world, on your terms. As the boss, you have to start by interviewing candidates, making some hires, and then continually evaluating how everyone is doing.

The media diet is a portfolio of sources with two main components: the lineup and tryouts.

Lineup

The lineup is the set of periodical media and other sources that have earned their place in your media diet and which you're most likely to stick with (though you always have the ability to let them go). These are your most valuable sources, and you must know exactly why you engage each of them. There are three types of sources in the lineup: stars, scans, and targets.

- *Stars:* These are the rare sources that consistently give useful, relevant information pertaining to one or more of your professional or personal interests. Stars are the sources most worth engaging (reading, viewing, or listening to), from beginning to end or close to it, on a regular basis. As such, they demand a good bit of time, so your media diet shouldn't contain many of them. In fact, depending on your available time and interest areas, you might do fine without any stars. In general, though, it's healthy to have one paper periodical and at least one website that fit this category. (Two of my stars are the print edition of *The Economist* and the popular website boingboing.net.)

- *Scans:* These comprise the majority of your lineup, perhaps three or four sources from a range of media types. Scans are sources that reliably deliver at least some relevant information. (My scans are the daily paper edition of the *New York Times* and a few websites and newsletters I read occasionally.) Scans are good either for engaging frequently for a subset of their content (as I do with the *Times*) or occasionally for all their content (as I do with some of the newsletters).

- *Targets:* These are sources that are good for a single targeted use. For example, you might subscribe to a competitor's newsletter just to read about their recent work. Or you may read a trade magazine to see if any of your clients or potential clients are mentioned, allowing you to send them a followup. When reading targets, be ready to clip: scissors for paper sources, copy and paste commands for bit-based sources.

The only way sources can make it onto a lineup is by going through the tryout phase.

Tryouts

Tryouts are sources that are not yet on the lineup, but are applying to be there. They must go through the tryout phase, almost like an extended job interview, in order to prove their worth for the media diet. Since a healthy media diet is as small as possible, it's likely that a given tryout will not be accepted onto the team. Still, it's worth continually being on the lookout for potential new sources to add. For example, I often try out newly launched trade publications (magazines and websites), just to make sure I don't miss any new, important voice in the field.

Some guidelines for tryouts:

- Be discerning about which sources to try out. The process takes time, so if you're confident that a source won't generate value, don't bother to try it.

- Be intentional: Know what you're trying out and why, and for how long you'll try it out. For a print publication, for example, I can generally tell within one issue what the viewpoint is, what the scope of information is, and whether it's worth adding to the media diet. Some sources may require trying out for two or three publishing cycles.

– Remember that the team can only be so big. Every addition to the lineup costs more of your precious resource of time, so you must be biased toward rejecting tryouts. And when you do move a tryout to the lineup, consider whether you can then remove one of the existing sources, so that the entire lineup stays around the same size.

It's also healthy to occasionally try an unusual or out-of-the-way publication, TV show, or radio show, as a one-off. You're not trying out the source for your permanent lineup; you're just reading, watching, or listening to it *once* to be open to a serendipitous encounter with an idea, trend, or person you wouldn't find in your normal sphere. If it ends up being good enough to add to your lineup, so much the better.

Maintenance

Maintaining a healthy media diet requires vigilance about what you're consuming. Thus it's important to constantly ask the question, "Is this worth my time?" at every level: the source ("Is this source worth my time?"), a particular issue of the source, an article, even down to the paragraph or section of an article you're in. If the answer is "no" to any of these, skip it. Move to the next article, or trash the entire issue; and if it happens too often with one source, consider removing it from the lineup altogether.

A balanced food diet draws proportionally on the various food groups; likewise, a healthy media diet draws on different kinds of sources. One good print news magazine can supply many of the basic nutrients, week after week, for keeping the user informed. Other sources, like trade publications, can fill the need for a specific view of the world. Even a tabloid—the nutrition-free, puffed-air-and-sugar confection of the media world—can occasionally be OK. The key, as always, is to limit the lineup to the smallest set of sources that keep you healthy and energized for the work you have to do. This means *not* consuming everything that comes your way.

Online media sources can present a special challenge because of the inconceivable number of choices. The Internet contains the biggest selection of media in history: millions of blogs, podcasts, videos, photo sets, and other sources. Techies often subscribe to a collection of such feeds with a tool called an "RSS reader," which allows them easy and instant access to dozens or hundreds of online sources. But the sheer amount of choice can be paralyzing. As one highly regarded blogger put it (on his blog, of course):

> I've collected so many RSS feeds that, when I sit down in front of the [RSS reader], it's almost as difficult a challenge as having no feed reader whatsoever. With dozens and dozens of subscriptions, each filled with dozens of unread posts, I often don't even know where to start.*

The explosion of online sources led me, a few years back, to propose "Hurst's Law": *An unbounded bitstream tends toward irrelevance.* (This devaluation of bits is apparent not just in the media diet but in other areas of bit literacy, and it will appear again in later chapters.)

There are valuable sources online, but bit-literate users have to be careful not to snack on lots of blogs "just because they're there." Ease of access does not imply value, and it's easy to waste time this way. Instead, users should apply the same tryout process on online sources as they would for any offline source. One or two well-chosen blogs—a handful at most—can usually cover what most users need; it's not productive to try to consume much more than that. (Techies who read blogs for fun, or as part of their own blog-writing process, will naturally consume many sources. But they make up a tiny minority of users.)

The bit-literate user is forever on a media diet and has to be in the habit of saying "no." There's too much to consume, and not enough time or attention to spend on even a fraction of it. Every possible source is a "no," unless it's proven otherwise in a disciplined tryout.

---

* Khoi Vinh writing on subtraction.com, November 29, 2006.

Know what you consume, and why, and be strict about evaluating what else to consume, especially online.

Identifying online sources

As any high school student should know, good research must be built on good sources. For generations, teachers, professors, and librarians have taught their students that you can't believe everything you read. Some sources are more reliable than others: the *Washington Post* is more reliable than the tabloids reporting on space aliens, and so on. The same discernment applies to the bit-literate media diet. However, bits often present a new challenge of identifying the source.

It's usually easy to find the name of any offline source. Many newspapers and magazines print their name and issue date on every page, and TV and radio shows usually identify themselves multiple times during a broadcast. Once the source is identified, the user can decide how reliable the content is. This is different with many online sources, though. When bits arrive—via e-mail or the Web—with partial or no context, it's easy to overlook the lack of a source and evaluate the content on its own merits. This causes problems.

A good example is the e-mail that gets forwarded endlessly—asking readers to sign a petition, forward the note to friends, or raise an alarm with the government. Either NPR is shutting down, or Congress is about to tax all Internet services, or KFC has stopped using real chicken in its food. Bit-illiterate users often forward these notes without ever noticing that a source isn't mentioned in the e-mail. E-mails like this look convincing, despite the lack of contextual clues that people are used to seeing in offline sources. The problem wouldn't occur in the offline world. It's unlikely, after all, that people would forward along the same claims if they were typed on a blank sheet of paper and tacked to the corkboard above the office water cooler, with no source mentioned.

Much more dangerous are e-mails that pretend to be from a reputable company, like eBay, but actually are intended to defraud the recipient of their credit card number or login information. An example below shows how to spot such messages.

Bit-literate users must know how to evaluate an online source. This may require more than just asking whether the source is reliable; online, it often means first determining what the source *is*. And that means reading a URL correctly.

How to read a URL

The source of any Web page is identified in the URL, or Web address, displayed in the address bar of the Web browser. It's also available before you get to a Web page, whenever you're about to click on a hyperlink to the page. If you hover the mouse pointer over a hyperlink, the Web browser should, in the lower-left of the window, show the URL of the page the link points to. (Many e-mails today also contain hyperlinks to Web pages.)

Each URL contains a "domain" that identifies the company, organization, or person hosting the Web page. Finding the domain thus equates to identifying the source of any Web page. Generally speaking, the domain is whatever appears just after any "http" and "www", and before the next slash. Here are some example URLs:

http://www.nytimes.com/pages/business/index.html
www.boingboing.net/archive.html
http://www.direct.gov.uk/Homepage/fs/en
goodexperience.com

The domains in the URLs above are nytimes.com, boingboing.net, direct.gov.uk, and goodexperience.com.*

---

* Domains are case-insensitive. That means that nytimes.com, NYTIMES.COM, and NYTimes.coM are all the same domain. However, everything in the URL to the *right* of the domain is case-sensitive. E-mail addresses, by the way, are completely case-insensitive: reader@example.com is the same address as Reader@EXAMPLE.com.

Now for a trickier example: what is the domain of this URL?

http://br.geocities.com/signin.ebay.com/SignIn.html

This is a misleading URL. It contains "ebay.com," but that's not the domain name—in fact, eBay has nothing to do with this page. The domain is geocities.com, which (by visiting geocities.com) one can see is a service that allows users to publish their own Web pages.

I once received an e-mail containing a similar URL. The e-mail's message text read, in part, "Respond to this question"—and then contained a big yellow "Respond Now" button. Everything in the e-mail looked like it came from eBay: the eBay logo, eBay-like colors and format, and no hint that this was concocted by a spammer. But by hovering the mouse over the Respond Now button, I saw a URL similar to the one above and immediately could tell that the message didn't originate from eBay. This confirmed my suspicion that it was a spam e-mail, pointing to a Web page that attempted to fool visitors into entering their account information.

The trickiest spam e-mails include a legitimate URL in their message body. Only on closer inspection can the user see that the link points to a completely different domain. For example, I frequently receive e-mails displaying the PayPal logo top and center, followed by this text:

> We recently noticed one or more attempts to log in to your PayPal account from a foreign IP address. If you recently accessed your account while traveling, the unusual log in attempts may have been initiated by you. However if you are the rightful holder of the account, click on the link below to log into the account and follow the instructions.
>
> https://www.paypal.com/us/cgi-bin/webscr?cmd=_login-run

The underlined text shows the paypal.com domain, but that's not where the link actually points. Hovering the mouse over the link shows a URL like this, in the lower-left of the browser window:

http://217-123-200-50.b2b.tiscali.it/.www.paypal.com/index.htm

Despite the existence of "paypal.com" in the URL, the domain is actually tiscali.it, proving that this is a fraudulent spam mail. When in doubt, hover the mouse over the link before clicking, and check where the URL points.

Discerning sources is useful for more than detecting spam mail. Anyone doing research online needs to know which sources are worth drawing upon. The same rule that students learned for years before the Internet applies here: if you don't know the source, or for any reason don't trust the source, then don't use it. Once you identify the domain of a Web page, regardless of what it might pretend to be, you can make a sound evaluation.

And that brings us back to e-mails that get forwarded endlessly, spreading rumors and hoaxes. E-mails are totally unreliable unless you know their source. If a coworker e-mails you, "the meeting has been rescheduled to 3pm," then that's reliable (or as reliable as the coworker is), since you know that your coworker originated the message. But if someone forwards you a "news clipping," petition, or alert, and there's no URL included as a source, immediately delete the e-mail.* If the URL is included, evaluate whether the domain is that of a reputable source, then click on the URL to make sure the source's website actually contains the information included in the e-mail. Whatever you do, never forward a message without a reliable source included. The best way to e-mail a news clip is to allow the recipient to verify the source. This requires a bit-literate way of sharing a clipping.

---

* If you want to confirm whether an e-mail is a hoax, check the "Urban Legends Reference Pages" at www.snopes.com.

Creating bit-literate clippings

A healthy media diet, comprised of reliable sources, constantly yields bits of information that are worth saving (for a project, say, or an informal scrapbook) or sharing with others. Everyone knows how to make a clipping of a paper-based source by using scissors; digital clippings require a different process.

Creating a text clipping in the bit-literate "clip format" means including the URL and other source information, as well as the article text itself. The whole clip can then be sent in the body of an e-mail or saved as a separate text file. (Text files are covered in more detail in the chapter on file formats.) In the clip, the following information should appear above the article text:

– *URL:* this is the most important field in the entire clip. The URL both gives the reader a way back to the story and identifies the source, if it's not listed elsewhere. The URL can be copied from where it appears in the Web browser, then pasted above the clip. If there is no usable URL—i.e., the page exists behind a "pay wall" or otherwise may not be accessible, then the publication and date are sufficient.*

– *Publication:* the name of the newspaper or other source. This can be left blank if it's obvious from the domain in the URL (e.g., nytimes.com).

– *Date:* this refers to the original publication date of the article, not today's current date or the e-mail's message-send date.

– *Title:* the title of the article.

– *Author:* the author of the article, if one is listed.

Below these identifying fields should lie the text of the article itself. Be sure to include the entire article, if the piece is spread across

---

* When clipping nytimes.com articles, an invaluable site is the "New York Times link generator," at http://nytimes.blogspace.com/genlink, which reveals special article URLs that do not expire or go behind a pay wall.

multiple Web pages. Some sites, like nytimes.com, have a "Print" or "Single Page" link that puts the entire article text on one page, which makes it easier to select the whole thing at once.

Paper-based clippings can be converted to bits in two ways: either by using a scanner to create an image of the printed clipping, or by finding the article text on the publisher's website. (Searching Google on the article title, in quotes, often brings up the article page.) Regardless of where clippings originate—in a paper-based source or online—it's best to store them in bits. Bits don't take up the physical space that paper clippings do, and they can be backed up, copied, and shared easily. And unlike paper, digital clips never age or deteriorate, as long as there's a reliable backup.

Once the clip is complete, it's time to share it or store it. The best way to share a text clipping is to paste it, in clip format, in the body of an e-mail—not as an attachment. Avoid sending a URL alone, since that puts the burden on recipients to find out what the page is, and why they should read it. One benefit of clip format, then, is that it's empathetic to the recipient.

Consider this example: often when I spot friends mentioned in the news, I e-mail them their article in clip format, so that they can then easily save it and forward it to their colleagues. The URL makes the source plainly visible and allows recipients to check the validity for themselves. If all I did was e-mail them "I saw you in the paper" or "read the story in the business section today," that would put all the responsibility on them to look up the article, and then find a way to save it or send it to friends. Many users don't know how to clip or share articles properly; sending them well-formatted clips saves them the trouble of muddling through the process themselves. Sending such an article in clip format shows that you respect the recipient's time—and that you maintain a good enough media diet to spot them in the news.

Some users prefer not to go to all the trouble of clip format and simply bookmark the URL of the online article, so they can refer to it later. (All Web browsers allow users to store bookmarks, or "favorites," and there are websites devoted to the same idea: del.icio.us and furl.net are two of the most popular.) But saving only a URL, and not the page contents, poses a risk: you're relying on an external website to store the clip for you. You have no guarantee that you'll be able to get back to those bits. A news article may go behind a pay wall after a few days, or the website could crash, or disappear, or change how articles are organized on the server, all of which would make the original article difficult or impossible to find again later. The best way to guarantee that you can access a clip again later is to save it, in clip format if possible, on your own computer.

Chapter 7: **Managing Photos**

Previous chapters explored how text has been transformed by the bit. E-mails have supplanted paper-based postal mail, digital todo lists have replaced paper checklists, and online news sources have begun to challenge traditional media. In each case, the unique attributes of bits have defined both the transformation and the bit-literate response. But bits have changed more things in our lives than just text. The visual, the graphic, and the photographic have transformed just as much.

Anyone born before 1990 will remember how people treated photographs before the age of bits. Every stage of a photo's life cycle was defined by one thing: cost. Film was expensive to buy and even more expensive to develop. Mistakes were costly, so chance was the enemy; everyone involved in the taking of a photograph acted accordingly. Taking a photo required posing everyone carefully, counting to three, and hoping that the shot came out. Only in extraordinary circumstances, like a wedding or family portrait, would more than one photo of the same subject be taken.

Once developed, almost all photos were kept—forever. Even mediocre photos were worth saving. Photos were expensive, after all, and the idea of throwing away any but the worst was nearly unthinkable. Most or all photos in a roll would find their way into a photo album, a proper showpiece for such precious items. The negatives had to be handled separately—held by the edges only!—and stored away in a cool, dark place, in case one of the photos was ever to be generated a second time.*

---

* For younger readers who are wondering, negatives were a kind of template from which one could order copies of a photo. Negatives showed reversed colors—white showed up as black, and so on—hence the name.

Film-based photographs were also costly in time: it took several days for a photo lab to develop the photos and deliver them back to the store for pickup. Admittedly, it was sort of fun to open up newly developed photos after waiting for several days—or longer, if the photographer was slow in sending the film to the lab. Polaroid made a huge advance with "instant cameras" whose photos developed within a couple of minutes when exposed to air. But the photo quality wasn't as good as regular film-based cameras, and there were no negatives with which to make copies. Polaroid solved the problem of time at the cost of quality, and the film was still expensive.

Bits have changed the equation in every way. Now in the twenty-first century, digital cameras offer immediacy *and* quality *and* low cost. The "film" is just bits—free, immediate, in infinite quantities—and scarcity is a thing of the past. Abundance is now the rule in photography, and bit literacy shows how to work accordingly.

Ironically, the abundance of bits brings with it a new challenge of scarcity. We covered it earlier with text bits, and it is just as relevant with photos: in an age of infinite bits, time and attention are the scarce resources. Time management is essential for working successfully with e-mail and todos. Similarly, managing photos requires being aware and intentional about how we spend our time and attention. For users who grew up with film-based cameras, the challenge of bit literacy is to change one's behavior.

Most people still do what they learned in the atomic era: taking one shot per subject, and never throwing away photos even if they're mediocre or bad. These practices made sense when film was expensive, but in the digital era they miss out on the advantages of bits—the ability to take many photos, and filter out bad ones, for no extra cost. Most users haven't learned bit-literate practices and are left with lower quality photos, since they rely on a single photo to capture a moment.

Other users take lots of photos, but they don't know where to put them. Photos spanning several months or years may lie in random locations on the computer in varying states of organization. For these users, a digital camera is just one more source of overload.

Photos and tags

The technology industry promises an easy fix to the organization problem by allowing users to enter "metadata" (literally, "data about data") about their photos. Some photo-organizing software, for example, allows users to rate each of their photos from zero to five stars. Users can thus save *all* their photos, duplicates and mediocre shots included, and presumably cut through the overload by simply sorting by rating. Other tools allow users to assign "tags," or descriptive keywords, to each photo. For example, a user might assign the tag "sunset" to a photo of a sunset; then, without having to navigate to any folder or through any hierarchy, she could then see all the photos bearing the "sunset" tag.

One drawback of metadata is that it can leave users dependent on one particular tool. After all, users are less likely to switch to a different tool—even a better one—if they've invested significant time entering ratings, tags, or other metadata in their current system. Bit-literate users need a system that avoids this dependence.

Another problem with metadata is that it's valuable only if users commit to entering it into all their photos. Tags, ratings, and other metadata require too much effort for regular, non-techie users who just want to organize their photos.* Some people might do it

---

* Tags in particular have received a lot of media hype, so it's worth a reality check. Tags *can* be genuinely valuable, but only if users use them consistently and accurately across a bitstream. For example, on the "social bookmarking" site del.icio.us, the mostly techie users consistently assign tags to Web pages they bookmark. In large quantities, such user-generated categorization can be very accurate. For example, searching del.icio.us on the tags "san francisco" and "food" yields more useful sites than from a similar search in most search engines. But this works only because del.icio.us has so many dedicated techie users who don't mind spending time adding tags to their bookmarks. In contrast, it's unlikely that an average user would expend such energy on their photo collection.

occasionally, and a tiny minority might do it enthusiastically, but the majority will store their photos unrated and untagged, which will leave them with a mountain of unorganized data.

This results in the pattern from the previous chapter: *an unbounded bitstream tends toward irrelevance.* I see this occasionally when people share photos (via e-mail or a photo-sharing website) without filtering them first. The photo set contains dozens or hundreds of mediocre shots, with many near-duplicates showing the same item, scenery, or posed group. It's tedious to look through. A dose of bit literacy, for the sender, would help a lot.

The bit-literate approach, as always, is to avoid overload by letting go of irrelevant bits—deleting, filtering, and pruning them—and then organizing what's left. The method may not be the easiest course of action in the short term, but the payoff is significant. The photos are higher quality, better organized, more easily shareable, and best of all, the bits are *yours.* You can access them when and where you want them, and you need not be afraid of changing computers, photo programs, or operating systems. When you're bit-literate, your bits are yours alone, and technology operates on your bits on your terms, or not at all.

Of course, users need to use *some* tools, and there are some good options available. But in the end, technology must function as a *tool,* not as a gatekeeper or owner of the bits. Users who take responsibility for their bits are free to take the bits elsewhere if they choose.

Bit literacy offers just such a system, which allows users to...

- navigate and find photos, and sets of photos, quickly and easily

- easily share a set of high-quality photos—via the Web, e-mail, or a slideshow on their computer

- avoid the extra work of entering ratings, tags, or other metadata into photos

– avoid being locked in to any particular software, tool, or company

– manage hundreds or thousands of incoming photos per year

I know that bit literacy fits these criteria because I've used the system for years to manage my own photos. Though I have thousands of photos going back over five years, I can usually find a given photo in seconds—without ever having entered metadata. (I manage my photos with Apple's iPhoto software, but if I ever need to, I can take them to Google's Picasa or some other service.)

The bit-literate photo management system has three steps: maximizing, filtering, and two-level storage.

1. Maximizing bits

The "film" in a digital camera is free, so there's no reason *not* to take lots of photos. In fact this is one case where it's bit-literate to accumulate lots of bits, initially. The old mindset, remember, was to take a few, tightly-controlled shots and then save nearly every print that got developed. In contrast, the bit-literate user should take many photos, in order to maximize the chances that one will be worth saving.

There are various ways to maximize bits when taking photos. For example, in a group shot: there's nothing wrong with posing and counting to three, but try taking shots the entire time. People often smile more naturally when they *don't* think a photo is being taken. When I take a photo of a group, I sometimes chatter like this: "OK, getting ready [click] for the shot, just one sec while I adjust this one thing [click], why didn't I ever learn how to use this crazy camera [click], OK, one, [click], two, three [click]. That's it, everybody! Thanks." Everyone thinks I've taken one photo, but I've taken five. Of course, this is difficult to keep up if there's a flash involved, but then I just ask people to be patient for a second or third shot "for insurance."

For practically any photo, in fact, I always try to take at least two shots. If my subject isn't a fast-moving object, and it's still in front of the camera after the first shot, I usually get an extra for insurance. If I'm not sure which angle looks good, I take multiple shots from multiple angles. If the lighting is strange, I may take shots both with and without a flash. The "film" is free, so I use every opportunity to increase my chances that one shot will come out well. I just have to commit to filtering out all but the best shot later.

2. Filtering

With multiple photos of every subject, we now must separate the wheat from the chaff. As stated earlier, users can't be expected to assign ratings, tags, or other metadata to their photos. Our system can scale to thousands of photos only if it's free from such demands on the user. But users have to expend *some* energy to filter their photos; if they don't, they'll be left with mediocre shots, or multiple near-duplicates, resulting in overload.

What do users have to do, then, to filter their photos *without* using tags or metadata? It's simple: let the bits go by deleting most of the photos they take. Consider that there are only two kinds of photos: the many to delete, and the very few to keep. Users need only make a single decision—yes or no—for each photo. (Think how much simpler that is than choosing from five possible star ratings, or worse, deciding what tag or caption to type into each photo.) The Delete button is elegant because it's permanent. Metadata might need re-entering if the bits move to another storage system, but once a photo is deleted, it's gone for good, and the user never has to worry about managing those bits ever again.

Filtering means deleting all the photos we don't want to keep, and that also means letting go of good pictures that are near-duplicates of others we will keep. Some users have difficulty with this. If there are two shots of dear Aunt Marge in the same pose, it's hard for some people to click the Delete button while Marge is smiling back at them on the computer screen. This gets easier with practice. Bit-literate users have to be quick, decisive, and ruthless with the Delete button (and not just with photos!). It doesn't matter how many pictures we take; it only matters which we keep.

Once we've taken our pass through the photos with the Delete button, the only photos remaining are the best shots—one per pose, one per scenic vista—with no duplicates or near-duplicates in the set. These filtered photos are now ready for sharing (by showing to others in slideshow mode, uploading onto a website, or e-mailing to friends). Recipients may comment, as friends sometimes do with me, that the photos are unusually good. The lighting, focus, pose, and people's expressions seem to come together for every single shot. But I'm not a great photographer; I'm just bit-literate. Because I maximize the bits by taking lots of photos, then filter ruthlessly, all I'm left with are unusually good pictures. The last step is to arrange the photos correctly.

3. Two-level storage

Even the most carefully filtered photos aren't worth much if users can't find them later. Without proper storage, they'll either join the disorganized clutter of other past photos or get lost somewhere else on the computer. Users must have *some* discipline for organizing photos. On the other hand, the system must require as little as possible of the user, which rules out entering metadata like tags and ratings.

The bit-literate system for organizing photos is based on "two-level storage." The key insight is that people can almost always find a given photo, or set of photos, by remembering when it was taken. This allows users to store all their photos within a two-level hierarchy:

[year] → [month-event]

Thus the top level of the photo collection is divided into years, as far back as the user's photos go. For example, I began taking digital photos in 2001, so the top level of my photo library is a series of folders named for years: 2001, 2002, 2003, and so on up to the present year. (I use Apple's iPhoto to create a library for each year and a separate program called iPhoto Library Manager to navigate between the years.*) Of course, I could just as easily move all my photos into Picasa, or any other photo program, as long as it allowed for two-level storage.

It's important to create the year folders manually so that you have full control over how you file your photos. Some tools such as iPhoto have a feature that automatically organizes photos by year, based on the creation date of the picture file. It's best to ignore this feature, since it's not always accurate. For example, if you scan a year-old photo print into the computer, iPhoto assigns it the date it was scanned, not the date the original photo was taken. Similarly, if someone e-mails you a photo, the creation date of the picture file is not necessarily accurate. The lesson here is not to allow computer-generated metadata to organize your photos. Only you, the user, should have say over where and how your photos are organized.

Within each year-library, I store photo sets in chronological order. The name of each photo set starts with its two-digit month number—01 through 12—followed by a keyword or phrase describing the set. In my photo library, there are two kinds of photo sets:

— Photos in ordinary, everyday circumstances at home or around New York City, where I live: these I put in folders with the descriptor "nyc" following the month number.

— Photos associated with a particular trip to a place outside New York, or a special occasion: these I put in folders with a

---

* Mac users can Google "iPhoto Library Manager" to find and buy the program. It's unfortunate that iPhoto is designed for one-level storage.

descriptor of the place ("maine") or occasion ("kelly's upstate wedding") after the month and date range.

Thus a given year's photo library may start with these folders:

01 nyc

02 nyc

0215-18 chicago

03 nyc

0308-9 kelly's upstate wedding

0331-0402 maine

04 nyc

05 nyc

...and they go on from there, ending with "12 nyc". Each of the folders contains one set of consistently good photos that I took during that month, in that place. (And they are all good photos, since I saved only the best shots from the many I took.)

The simplicity of two-level storage has two benefits:

— It doesn't require much from the user. Perhaps once or twice a month, the user creates a new folder, names it with a month number and a descriptor, and drags the filtered photos into it. Once a year the user creates a new year folder. That's all.

— It's easy to find photos later, because there aren't many places a given photo could be. Reducing the possible places where bits can reside is just as important as any other aspect of storing them.

It's very easy to go back to find, say, the vacation photos from last summer, or the photos of the trip to Denmark two years ago. Even if I don't remember the month of a given event, I can quickly scan the folders from that year—there are usually not many more than twenty—to find the right one. And this is why it's important to have two levels of storage. A one-level storage system would mean that every photo set I've ever taken would sit in the same list. This wouldn't scale, because after a couple of years the list of folders would stretch far down the page, making it difficult to scan. A two-level system, on the other hand, scales nicely. Each year contains a modest list of folders, and the list of years won't get very long for twenty years or more.

To be fair, two-level storage won't work for everyone, under all circumstances. For example, a professional photographer with dozens of photo sets a month might find it too lightweight to be practical. A high-tech user with an obsessive need to input lots of metadata would find it unsatisfying. But this system, like bit literacy overall, is helpful for the great majority of users who just want to organize their bitstreams in a simple way. Most people have a reasonably small number of digital photos to handle and would find this an infinitely better system than a jumble of photos stored haphazardly on the computer.

One other benefit of this system is that, because all the photos live in one place, it's easier to back up an entire photo collection (or transport them to another service). The "other essentials" chapter describes how to back up files, but it's worth making the point here because of the importance of photos. Losing one's documents can be a real problem, but losing one's photos can be devastating. Keep your photos well-organized and back them up regularly.

Simplicity is the key to bit-literate photo management. Tags and other metadata are purely optional. Users don't even need to enter captions or names for their photos. Except for taking lots of photos, filtering them, and moving the good ones into the right folder, there's no other interaction that bit-literate users need in order to properly organize their photos. With this tiny amount of discipline, users can finally take control of their photo bits.

Chapter 8: **Creating Bits**

If you have to say something, keep it short.

Any bit-literate discussion about creating bits—text, photos, audio, or anything else—must first acknowledge one glaring truth: we have plenty of bits already. Every time you send an e-mail, take a picture, or create a Web page, you're adding drops into an ocean that's plenty deep enough. Are you sure your message is important enough to add? If so, then at least be empathetic to the recipient. Create the bits in a way that will deliver your message without adding to the overload that the recipient may already be experiencing.

The core statement of bit literacy, "let the bits go," is amply relevant when creating bits. Being effective and empathetic means delivering the message in as *few* bits as possible, letting go of all the other possible bits that could be included. After all, the more bits a message contains, the more time and attention it requires for the recipient to get through it. Shorter is better.

This isn't a new idea, of course. Books on good writing have always encouraged brevity. Strunk and White's classic *The Elements of Style* put it best: "Omit needless words." What's different today, though, is the vastly decreased amount of time people have to read, watch, or listen. There are too many bits, and too little time, so brevity is now more than a suggestion. It is essential.

To be clear, the goal of brevity isn't to conserve computer memory, or somehow to go easy on the "plumbing" in the network. For all but the biggest files, there's plenty of bandwidth to transmit them across the Internet, and plenty of hard drive space to store them when they arrive. Hardware today is powerful and abundant, and it's getting more so all the time. What's scarce is the time and attention of the people who are receiving the message. A bit-literate message, in any form, is respectful of that scarce resource. This means:

- When writing an e-mail, be short and to the point.

- When displaying photos, only show the best ones—never duplicates or bad shots.

- When creating a website, make sure the point of the site is clear from the first glance of the home page.

There are many other kinds of bit-based messages for which the same rule applies. In all cases, the constant question should be "Is this necessary?", asked at every level: "Is this paragraph necessary? This word? This pixel?" The bits in any message—whether textual, visual, or otherwise—should be as few as necessary to deliver the message.

We've touched on this idea in previous chapters. The photos chapter, for example, showed how to filter photos. The media diet chapter showed how to say "no" when invited to engage new bitstreams. Whether creating or receiving bits, the goal of bit literacy is to omit all irrelevant bits so that the ones that remain are worth spending time on. You must always create bits with that goal, acting on behalf of the person (perhaps you) who will have to engage those bits later.

Two concepts are useful to know here: frontloading and structure.

Frontloading the content

Frontloading could also be called "first things first": always deliver the point of the message as *early* as possible. This guideline can be applied to any bit-type, but the most relevant is e-mail. Recipients have an overabundance of e-mail messages, with new ones constantly arriving, so it's especially important when writing an e-mail to frontload the point of the message. Practicing this concept in e-mail will then translate naturally to any other bits you create.

When an e-mail arrives in the inbox, the first thing the user sees is the Subject line. If the Subject line is not empathetic to the recipient's scarce time and attention, it might be the *only* part of the e-mail he reads before moving on to the next message. To maximize the chance that he'll read the body of the message, the sender should frontload the content. This starts with writing a Subject line that is fully descriptive, as early as possible, and is as short as possible.

For example, consider this Subject line:

```
Subject: Everything you need to know about the upcoming
meetings in Chicago
```

Even though the Subject is descriptive as a whole, it's "backloaded"; the reader can only get the point of it by reading all eleven words. Rewriting the Subject to frontload it, we get:

```
Subject: Chicago meetings: schedule, agenda, directions
```

This revised Subject is more descriptive with fewer words. It frontloads the most descriptive text ("Chicago meetings"), and only then moves on to secondary items ("schedule, agenda, directions").

The content in the body of an e-mail should also be frontloaded. It should plainly state the point of the message early on—usually in the first sentence after the greeting—and be as short as possible. In other words:

– State the most important idea first.

– State the second most important idea second.

– If there's a third most important idea, consider whether it needs to be in the message at all.

– End the message as soon as possible.

The length of an e-mail is important. The less time a message takes to read, the more likely it is to be read.* This also means avoiding e-mail attachments if possible. Writing the entire message in the body of an e-mail allows the recipient to see it all in one place, instead of having to open a separate application. (Attachments are discussed further in the file formats chapter.)

Similarly, when sending a news clipping, as discussed in the media diet chapter, it's best to send the entire text of the article along with the URL, instead of just the URL with no descriptive language. Even though that lengthens the e-mail, it's easier for the user to see the point of the e-mail than if they had to click the URL to see what it was about.

The hook and support

Before describing bit-literate message structure, we must define some terms. First, rather than continually mentioning "the most important idea" or "the point of the message," which are rather wordy, I prefer "the hook." This term is helpful shorthand for a concept that bit-literate users apply constantly while creating bits. The hook is the main idea of the entire message—in an e-mail, a presentation, or any other document. (In different contexts it may be known as the crux, the thesis, or the "nut.") In fact, any chunk of information—a Subject line, a paragraph, a Web page—can and usually should contain a hook.

Frontloading, then, means stating the hook as soon as possible. And then the message should end as soon as possible. But there's a step missing. What happens between the hook and the end of the message? The missing piece is the "support," which is any information needed to explain or back up the hook. A support might be necessary, for example, if the hook is provocative,

---

* Personal letters are one exception. Often, for letters from close relatives or traveling friends, "the longer, the better."

requiring the reader to be convinced of its validity, or if the hook is obscure or for any reason needs clarification or explanation.

Thus, to be empathetic to the recipient, an e-mail should be structured in the following sequence:

– Subject, with frontloaded hook

– Greeting

– Hook (restated)

– Support

– End

(Of course, some e-mails might not need a greeting or a support. In fact, in certain instances an e-mail with *only* a Subject, and no message body, might suffice. Whatever elements are present, though, should follow the sequence above.)

The support may contain multiple statements or arguments, so it's important to present it clearly. A big block of text is generally the wrong way to do it. Text bullets—comprised of a hyphen and a space—provide a much better way of displaying multiple elements of the support.

Example: Rewriting an e-mail

Now for an example that puts it all together. Consider the e-mail below:

```
From: John Smith (john@example.com)
To: Steve Doe (steve@example.com)
Subject: Announcement about the finance department's
change to the 401k plan


Hi,
As you all know, the company offers a 401k plan to all
employees via AcmeOne Investing. There are many ways to
```

gain value in your retirement account through this tax-deferred instrument. We have just made some changes to the plan, including offering a dozen more mutual funds, and new tracking tools on the website. But even better, we have just started a new matching policy where the company will match up to 5% of your contributions. You can start this whenever you want by filling out some forms at my desk. The deadline to get the first month's matching contribution is December 7.

Thanks,
-John

At first glance it may look harmless enough, but the e-mail contains several problems:

- The Subject line is unnecessarily long and doesn't frontload the hook.

- In fact, the Subject fails to mention the hook at all, which is an important action item. If employees fill out the forms by December 7, they can get the first month's matching contribution.

- The body leads with the support in a big block of text and hides the hook in the last sentence. Note how each sentence is more important than the last: a good example of backloading.

Seeing the long Subject line, employees might ignore the message, especially if it's one of dozens or hundreds of e-mails in their inbox. Even if they do open the e-mail, they'll see the big block of text and might not read the whole thing. The first sentence makes it look like a standard office FYI that they can safely ignore. Overlooking the action item buried in the last sentence, they will probably fail to fill out the new forms. Because of the poor structure of the e-mail, employees may miss one or more matching contributions, and John may have to send more e-mails to follow up on this one.

This is a small example, but multiplied by the millions of such e-mails that get sent every day in companies and organizations around the world, it's indicative of the staggering loss of productivity due to poor e-mail structure. On the bright side, these pitfalls are easy to avoid. Creating a bit-literate e-mail doesn't require any special technology, just proper training and some empathy for the recipient.

Rewriting the e-mail, we get:

From: John Smith (john@example.com)
To: Steve Doe (steve@example.com)
Subject: Please fill out forms by Dec. 7 for new 401k match

Hi Steve,

Please come by my office by December 7 to fill out a couple of 401k forms. This will start the company matching your monthly contributions to your 401k account. (You can fill out the forms later, but to get the first month's contribution, I need the forms by December 7.)

FYI, the company has made several changes to our 401k account with AcmeOne Investing:

— The company will now match up to 5% of your contributions, once you sign up

— A dozen more mutual funds are available

— There are new tracking tools on the website

All other aspects of the plan are the same.
Thanks,
— JS

Notice all the elements of bit-literate e-mail structure:

- *Subject, with frontloaded hook:* The entire Subject is the hook, and its wording is frontloaded. If Steve, the recipient, scans even the first three words—"Please fill out"—he'll understand that there's a todo in this e-mail, and that he should keep reading.

- *Greeting:* This e-mail greets Steve by name, which makes it more likely he will read the message. (Depending on the sender's e-mail program, this may be difficult when mailing a large number of recipients, but it's good to include if possible.)

- *Hook (restated):* The message body has more space than the Subject line, so it can be a little more verbose, if it makes things clearer. Here the first paragraph explains the hook in more detail.

- *Support:* Using text bullets, the support lists the changes to the 401k account, leading with the most important change: the new matching policy.

- *End:* Although there might be other, less relevant details that could fit into this message, John omits them in order to finish the message. The shorter the message, the more likely Steve will read it and complete the todo, saving John from followup.

This structure applies to more e-mails than just todos, as in the example above. An FYI message, without an action item, still has a hook. For example, if the message above was merely *announcing* a new corporate-matching policy, the e-mail might center around a hook like, "The company now matches your 401k contributions up to 5%, and you're already enrolled in the program."

Bit-literate message structure

E-mail is a natural medium for structuring bits around a hook, but it's not the only one. Much of Web design, for example, can be brought back to the same idea. Each Web page should have one primary purpose—its hook—and the page design should frontload that hook. This means stating the purpose of the page most prominently—top and center, usually—with no other competing text, links, or other interface elements distracting the user. Secondary items supporting the hook can then appear below; optional unrelated items can appear in surrounding columns. Overall, the better structured a Web page, and the fewer chunks of information it contains, the more understandable and useful it is—and the more people will use it.

There is, in fact, a bit-literate way to structure *any* digital message: an e-mail, a Web page, a PowerPoint, or any other document. The hook should appear near the beginning, after any necessary context is set; and the support, if it exists, should follow. The support should end as soon as possible, perhaps finishing with a pointer to an appendix with more detailed information.

These are the components of bit-literate message structure:

- Context
- Hook
- Support
- Optional appendix

The hook and support are discussed above; thus, the context and optional appendix are described in more detail below.

Context

Computer scientist Alan Kay once wrote that people only learn in relation to something they already understand. This is a brilliant insight that applies broadly to teaching and design, but also to the construction of any bit-literate message. The first job of a communicator is to ensure, before delivering the message, that the recipient has the right context.

Context is naturally present in many media. Printed newspapers, for example, give physical cues—the front page, the section headings and dividers, the date at the top of every page—that set the framework for the reader to understand the content of the articles. Online, e-mails have the advantage of basic context built in, displaying the date and sender's name before the message starts. (A well-written Subject line might also be considered a part of the context, before the body delivers the full-fledged hook.)

Many bit-based documents, however, do not have the advantage of natural context, and so it often needs to be added. When creating such documents, users must ensure that they set context before getting to the hook. This means starting with the following:

- document title

- author's name

- date (of this particular version of the document; it should match the date in the file name, as described in the "naming files" chapter)

- optional "preface": anything necessary to explain why this document was created, or to catch people up (e.g., for a deliverable in the middle of a long project)

For example, documents like memos and reports should begin by listing the author, date, and title before (optionally) continuing to a preface, and then delivering the hook.

Perhaps the best example of the need for context is the PowerPoint file. Often people create PowerPoints without including basic context: who created the presentation, when, for whom, and most importantly, *why*. This information should be delivered in the first few slides before revealing the hook of the document. For example, at my consulting company when we create a PowerPoint file for a client, we often start with the following slides:

- Slide 1: Title slide (containing document title, date, client name, our company name, and contact info)
- Slide 2: Table of contents listing sections of the document
- Slide 3: Project goal (stated simply, in one or a few bullets)
- Slide 4: Project overview (showing all phases of the project, and noting which is the current phase)
- Slide 5: Section divider introducing the hook (e.g., "Project strategy"), allowing the consultant—during the actual presentation—to make sure everyone is fully caught up on the context and has no questions before proceeding to the hook
- Slide 6: The hook

The first five slides serve as context; the fifth and sixth deliver the hook. From there the document moves into the support and possibly includes an appendix at the end.

Optional appendix

Sometimes a bit-literate message is fully fleshed out in its context, hook, and support, and yet there is still some data that could be useful to a smaller audience that wants more detail. This calls for an appendix, a set of information included, or referenced, at the end of the support. If it was part of the support it would harm the message by making it too long, but it's appropriate to offer elsewhere, where it can be valuable to any recipients who seek it out.

In e-mail, a good way to add an appendix is to finish the note with a pointer to more information. In our 401k example above, this sentence could be added at the end of the message: "The entire 401k plan documentation is listed on the AcmeOne website at this URL: ...."

The appendix is also useful in PowerPoint presentations. At my consulting firm, we usually end the support with a final "thank you" slide, so that the audience knows that the presentation is complete. The very next slide, though, is a title slide that reads "Appendix," after which any extra slides can be pasted—building out deeper layers of the support, or offering tangentially related data or analysis.

Other thoughts on creating bits

Here are a few final guidelines on creating bits, especially in e-mail.

— *State the obvious.* Avoid ambiguity, even if it means making the message a little longer. If written right, an e-mail should deliver its message without the recipient having to ask for clarification. If the message is ambiguous, either the recipient will ask a question, which slows down the process, or worse, the recipient *won't* ask a question and possibly misinterpret the message.

— *Avoid relative dates.* The words "today" and "tomorrow" can be confusing or misleading in e-mail. Since you have no control over when the recipient opens the message, it's essential to be clear when talking about time. No matter where the recipient is, in the next office or across the world, always use absolute dating. Write "today, Wednesday" or "tomorrow, Thursday." If you want to be extra clear, state the whole date: "today, Tuesday, February 12." (Obviously, if the message references a time of day and the recipient is in a different time zone, specify the time zone as well.)

— *Remember that bits are everywhere and forever.* An important rule of thumb, and not just in e-mail: don't ever create bits that you wouldn't want broadcast to the entire world. Any thoughtless, offensive, or otherwise poorly worded message dashed off in a moment can be saved, passed around, reported on, posted worldwide, and even brought up in a courtroom. Bits that are meant to be private sometimes have a way of getting out. The instantaneous and timeless nature of bits makes them dangerous to create, ever, if you don't want them shared.

— *Never e-mail angry.* Abraham Lincoln had a wise policy about letters he wrote when he was angry: he would put them in his desk and never send them. That was during an era when it took more time to create and send a message; today it's a lot easier to send an angry message before you can reconsider. It's important to have a personal policy: if you feel angry when you write an e-mail, save it as an unsent draft and give yourself some time to "cool off" before deciding whether to send it.

E-mail is generally a poor medium for emotion or subtle cues. It's no accident that many users still sprinkle their e-mails with emoticons, like :) and ;) , to help clarify that an otherwise risky statement is meant as "just kidding." Almost any other medium is more precise at subtle cues: phone calls have tone of voice, video can show body language, handwritten notes are expressive in the strokes of the pen, and in-person, face-to-face communication is still—and always will be—best of all. E-mails are great at keeping up with details and increasing productivity, but they're not as good at the "soft stuff." It's yet one more reason to let the bits go: finishing your bit-based work allows you get to *real* life offline.

Chapter 9: **File Formats**

It's easy to overlook the importance of file formats. Everything in the method described up to this point, in fact, can be accomplished without knowing much about them. For example, the chapter on organizing photos never mentions the most common digital photo format, JPG, or why it's the most popular. People can organize their photos, after all, without knowing what format the pictures are in. Still, as this chapter will show, file formats are essential to bit literacy.

A file format is the particular arrangement of bits in a photo, song, document, or any other digital file. The format is usually denoted by a three-letter abbreviation, or "extension," at the end of the file name. (For example, a photo named "picture1.jpg" has the extension "jpg", which refers to the JPG file format.) Many users can recognize common extensions—.doc files are created by Microsoft Word, .ppt files by PowerPoint, and so on—but are otherwise unaware of file formats.

Bit-literate users must have this awareness. File formats aren't arbitrary or random in their makeup; to the contrary, they are intentionally designed items, just like cars, chairs, and other consumer products. Every file format has certain assumptions and goals "baked" into its design, so it may or may not be helpful in a given circumstance. Some formats are built for easy shareability, others for professional-grade accuracy, and yet others are designed in part to advance the goals of the company that owns them.

It's up to the user to choose the best format. The moment of choice usually comes when users create bits, either to share with others or to save for themselves. There's an important distinction to make: the previous chapter covered how to create the content of a message, but here we discuss which format to put it in. Imagine a smitten poet who knows just the thoughts and feelings he wants to express in a love poem, but hasn't yet chosen the language to write it in. Choosing a widely understood language like English could be a good choice, while writing it in Klingon would narrow the appeal considerably (unless his lover is a die-hard Trekkie). The choice of language is important, even though it doesn't change the thoughts that the poet wants to express. Similarly, any file format could be a better or worse choice to contain a given message.

When creating bits, users must consider which file format will...

- contain the message with an acceptable level of quality

- allow recipients to download the file quickly and open it easily

- be compatible with the most computers and devices, both today and in the future

Choosing the best format—and there often is a choice—allows users to create, receive, and otherwise engage the bits as easily and freely as possible. So while it's not necessary to learn about every single file format in use, it's vital for the bit-literate user to know about the most common formats for images, audio, and text, all of which are covered below.

Image file formats

One of the most popular image formats is JPG, also known as JPEG, with the file extension .jpg and pronounced "jay-peg." JPG was designed to work with images with many different colors and gradations of color. To minimize the amount of storage space an image requires, JPG compresses information wherever there is a gradual change in color. This makes JPG the best format for *photographic* images. Indeed, most digital cameras use the JPG format by default, so many users create JPG images without knowing it.

JPG is *not* a good choice, however, for images that need clear, distinct lines or color differences. Logos, line art, and icons tend to look blurry in JPG due to its compression, but they look much better in the other two common image formats: PNG and GIF.*
PNG is pronounced "ping" or "p-n-g," and GIF is pronounced like "gift" without the "t", though some people say "jif." Unless you're a Web designer or other creative professional, you're unlikely to create PNG or GIF images; doing so usually requires an image-editing program. (One exception is the built-in screenshot function on Macintosh computers, which creates PNG images.) What's important to know is that PNG and GIF create smaller files than JPG for images with clean lines, while JPG creates smaller files than PNG and GIF for photographic images.

The key difference between image formats is *file size:* the smaller an image file is in a given format, the better, because it takes up less memory and downloads faster for recipients. (Note that this is different from simply resizing an image to different dimensions, akin to framing a smaller version of an original painting. Resizing photos is covered in the "other essentials" chapter.) Stated another way, users should choose the format that requires the fewest bits to communicate the message. Elegance, brevity, simplicity: these are the qualities of a good file format.

Audio file formats

File size is also the key difference in audio. The most popular audio format is MP3 (pronounced "m-p-three"), with the file extension .mp3. An MP3 file is a compressed version of the original audio recording, so its sound isn't quite as good as a store-bought CD, but the worldwide popularity of MP3 indicates that the quality

---

* PNG and GIF are nearly interchangeable formats. In the late 1990s GIF was used widely on the Internet until Unisys, a technology company, began to enforce its software patent on the GIF format. PNG, a similar format with no patent protection, then became very popular. When the Unisys patent expired in 2003, GIFs became freely available again. Today the only major difference between the formats is that a GIF file can contain an animated graphic.

is good enough for most users. Users choose MP3 because the quality is acceptable and the files download quickly. (Like JPG, in fact, many people use MP3 without knowing it. Most tools for "ripping" and "burning," for transferring songs from CD to computer and back, use MP3 by default.)

Professionals who need to work with original audio, like composers and editors, often work in other audio formats. Two of these are WAV (.wav), pronounced "wave," and AIFF (.aiff), pronounced "a-i-f-f"—full-sized, uncompressed file formats for audio. They have better sound quality than MP3—in fact, they can match the quality of a store-bought CD—but they are much bigger, so they're less practical to share. A three-minute song in AIFF format could take up ten times the space (and hence download time) of an MP3 file containing the same song.

Thus the key criteria of file formats for audio and images are quality and size. Whichever format contains the message, at acceptable quality, in the fewest bits, is the best choice.

There's one aspect to audio formats, however, that doesn't exist in image formats: corporate ownership. The music industry, concerned about the easy shareability of MP3 files, has created audio file formats that use "digital rights management," or DRM, to make duplication difficult.

One example of an audio format with DRM is AAC, with the extension of .m4p, best known as Apple's format for songs on its online iTunes music store. AAC is a compressed music format, much like MP3, but the DRM included in the format creates restrictions on copying, sharing, and even playing via non-Apple software.* DRM is a complex topic; the point here is that file formats can be designed for the benefit of the corporation, not just the user. This becomes even more apparent in text formats.

---

* For more details on AAC, see the Wikipedia entry for "Advanced Audio Coding."

Text formats: e-mail

Whether you know it or not, every time you write an e-mail, compose a letter, draft a memo, or otherwise create digital text, you choose a format for the text. Just as with images and audio, text formats offer better and worse choices, depending on the situation. Choosing the right text format is especially important, though, since it's the medium users do most of their work in.

As an example of the importance of text formats, consider the e-mail below:

```
From: John Smith (john@example.com)
To: Steve Doe (steve@example.com)
Subject: Meeting agenda
Attachment: agenda.doc


Hi Steve,
Attached is the agenda for today's meeting.
-John
```

Here John has sent Steve an e-mail referencing an attached Word document. The only function of the e-mail text is to ask Steve to read the attachment. Opening agenda.doc, Steve sees four lines of text:

Meeting Agenda:

- Review of last meeting
- Check-ins with team members
- New business

The content of the Word document is fine; it's the file format that is problematic. Because John put the agenda in a Word document, Steve can only access it by taking several steps:

— double-clicking the attachment icon

— waiting for Microsoft Word to load, if it's not open already

- reading the document, once it's open (while ignoring the rulers, margins, toolbars, menus, and other items that Microsoft packs into the user interface surrounding the text)

- closing the document

- clicking to get back to the e-mail program

Obviously, it would have been more efficient for John—and *much* more efficient for Steve, the recipient—to skip Microsoft Word and type the meeting agenda directly into the body of the e-mail, like this:

```
From: John Smith (john@example.com)
To: Steve Doe (steve@example.com)
Subject: Meeting agenda


Hi Steve,


Here is the agenda for today's meeting.
- Review of last meeting
- Check-ins with team members
- New business


-John
```

Consider the advantages of sending that message, instead of an attached Word document:

- It's faster and easier for John to write the e-mail, because he doesn't have to open Word or attach a document to the e-mail.

- It's faster and easier for Steve to read the e-mail, because he doesn't have to open Word to read the agenda, and then switch back to the e-mail program.

- Steve can read the message on any device that reads e-mail, regardless of whether it runs Microsoft Word.

Sending the message this way is more efficient for both sender and receiver, and it's compatible with more technology. This demonstrates the three qualities—elegance, brevity, and simplicity—that define the best choice of format.

There's one other advantage to putting text in the body of an e-mail rather than in a Word document: file size. Similar to image and audio formats, one way to evaluate a text format is to measure how many bits it takes to express a given message. John's note above serves as a good example. Sent in the body of an e-mail, the message takes up 122 bytes. (It takes eight bits, or one byte, to contain each character in the message.) Using Word to type in *just* the meeting agenda, not the greeting or signoff, creates a file that weighs in at almost 20 kilobytes, or 20,000 bytes—a more than hundredfold increase in memory to hold the same message.[1]

Text formats: Word

One may rightly wonder why Word would create such a bloated file for a simple message. The answer is that Microsoft Word isn't designed to create digital text at all. It's designed to create *paper.*

When Word launched in the mid-1980s, personal computers weren't much more than glorified typewriters. There was no e-mail or Internet access for most users, so practically the only reason people typed *anything* was to print it on paper. Word became one of the most popular "desktop publishing" tools, offering features that had historically been accessible only to professional print shops: fonts, rulers, layout, and so on.[2]

---

1 Test conducted on Microsoft Word 2004 for Mac, version 11.0.

2 This was the first time many computer users had ever encountered fonts. The term "ransom note" took on a new meaning around this time as many Word users created Christmas letters, neighborhood newsletters, and other documents with every other sentence printed in a different font, size, and style.

Two decades later, Word remains much the same program. Although it has many more features, at its heart Word is still a tool designed to create paper printouts of formatted text. It's no coincidence that, in some versions of Word, the first thing users see when opening a new document is a pair of inch-scale rulers on the top and left of the screen. The rulers refer only to the length of the sheet of paper that will be printed. It's an anachronism in the digital age.*

Admittedly, global corporations print more paper today than ever before. Often this is due to the lack of bit literacy training; sometimes users print because they don't know how to organize digital files or share them online. Like other unproductive practices discussed in earlier chapters, these will naturally be resolved as more users begin to practice bit literacy. A completely "paperless office" is probably unachievable for most companies, but they certainly can reduce their paper consumption from current levels.

In the meantime, there are exceptional situations when text *does* need to be printed on paper. The most common instance I see of this is the legal contract, which needs to be printed in order to get a signature. The sections and sub-sections of contractual language also lend themselves to Word's formatting abilities, and most lawyers tend not to work much with other tools. But beyond such exceptions, there is little reason for average users to turn their digital text into paper. Creating and sharing text in bits is faster, easier, cheaper, more environmentally friendly, and overall better than churning out pressed trees and chemicals. In the digital age, Word is usually the wrong choice for text.

Another problem with Word is its multiple incompatible versions. It's most accurate to talk about Word document *formats*, since

---

* A particularly irritating reminder of paper arrived in the late 1990s when Microsoft added "Clippy," an animated paper clip, to Word and the other applications in Microsoft Office. It would pop up, unannounced and uninvited, and "helpfully" suggest what the user might like to do next. The gratuitous intrusion on users' productivity was so universally loathed by users worldwide that Microsoft removed Clippy, or at least silenced it by default, within a few years.

every new version of Word (arriving, it seems, every couple of years) comes with its own, slightly different Word file format. Previous versions of Word are unable to open files in newer Word formats, giving customers a strong motivation to buy upgraded versions of Word, regardless of whether they actually want any of the new features. Microsoft has used this "lock-in" effect for years to help sell millions of copies of Office, the "productivity suite" that includes Word. The *Wall Street Journal* recently reported on the newly released Office 2007: "Microsoft has also changed the standard file format for Office files. Older versions of Office, on both Windows and Macintosh computers, won't be able to read these new file types without special conversion software."*

This raises the question of what *is* the best file format for digital text. If Word documents are bloated and inefficient, what's the alternative? Users need something more specific than "text in the body of an e-mail," especially since a lot of text is created outside e-mail. Fortunately, users have just such a format. In fact they've always had it, as long as computers have existed. It's called ASCII.

Text formats: ASCII

ASCII, pronounced "ASK-ee," corresponds roughly to the letters, digits, and symbols on a computer keyboard: a through z, in both lowercase and uppercase, digits 0 through 9, and most standard punctuation marks. Text created from these characters is known as ASCII text, and any file comprised only of ASCII characters is an ASCII file. (The meaning of the acronym ASCII isn't important, but in case you want to impress a techie, it stands for American Standard Code for Information Interchange.)

ASCII is the simplest possible text format because it's made up of text characters only. (For that reason, ASCII is also known as "plaintext.") ASCII files contain no fonts, styles, colors, or

---

* "Bold Redesign Improves Office 2007," by Walt Mossberg, the *Wall Street Journal*, January 4, 2007: http://ptech.wsj.com/archive/ptech-20070104.html

formatting—just the text. That's why an ASCII message is so much smaller than a Word document containing the same text; Word documents include print-related data.

ASCII also predates Microsoft Word, having been developed for the nascent Internet of the 1970s and 1980s.* ASCII's simple format was valuable because bandwidth was so scarce. (Today's Word files would have been impossibly large.) These days, just about every device that reads digital text *at all* reads ASCII. Computers, PDAs, cell phones, even Microsoft Word itself—everything that deals with text reads ASCII. It hasn't gotten a lot of press, and no one got rich from inventing it, yet the ASCII format has become one of the most useful and widespread digital technologies ever created.

The two text formats are near-opposites, in fact: ASCII is small, elegant, and compatible with everything; Word is heavy, slow, and proprietary. Much like the DRM-enabled AAC audio format, the Word format is designed with the profit motive in mind. Microsoft is the sole owner of the Word format, so no software application is supposed to read or write the Word format unless Microsoft authorizes it. (Other tools like Google Docs can do so only because their engineers have "reverse-engineered" the format to make their software compatible.) This is in contrast to ASCII, which is a publicly owned, freely available standard that has been in use for decades.

Creating ASCII

Most users create ASCII text, even if they're not aware of doing so, whenever they write an e-mail. All e-mail programs have the ability to create ASCII text, and many do so by default. (Most PDAs, cell phones, and other text-enabled devices send messages in ASCII, too.)

---

* The movie *The Matrix* gives a nod to ASCII, as the protagonists' computers show a constant stream of green-on-black characters—a familiar sight to anyone who used computers before the mid-1980s.

But creating ASCII doesn't always mean sending an e-mail. Sometimes users just want to create text—taking meeting notes, for example—to save or share, but not necessarily to print. This calls for a program that is focused on creating and saving text files, not e-mailing them. This is a *text editor*, an application built specifically to create ASCII text files. There are multiple choices for every platform:

– Mac users should use TextWrangler (a program by Bare Bones Software) or the TextEdit program included on most Macs today.

– Windows users should use metapad, TextPad, or for more advanced users, UltraEdit. Searching Google on any of the names will bring up the appropriate website.

– Linux users already know their favorite text editor.*

Text editors allow the user to create, edit, and save ASCII files, which come with all the advantages of the format. It's a free, non-proprietary format that works and shares equally well on all platforms. An ASCII file created on a Mac will show the same text on a Windows PC, a BlackBerry, or on any other device.

It's worth noting that even Microsoft Word can create ASCII text. (To save any Word document as an ASCII file, click "Save As" and then save the document in "Text Only," or .txt, format.) Thus, in a sense, Word itself is a text editor. But Word's menagerie of distracting menus, toolbars, popup windows, and print-related features make it harder to use than a text editor like TextWrangler, which was specifically designed for text editing.

Peeking inside a Word document

There's one last comparison to make between ASCII and Word format. The earlier example noted that a Word file is over a

---

* In the Un*x world, emacs is the one true text editor. (No letters, please! Just tweaking vi users.) Ahh, geek humor.

hundred times bigger than an ASCII file containing the same text. Any good text editor, like TextWrangler, can show the reason why. Opening the Word file containing the meeting agenda reveals the contents of the file:

```
-ø†°±·›,`  ! ■.˘˘˘
˘˘˘˘˘˘˘˘˘˘˘˘˘˘˘˘˘˘˘˘˘˘˘˘˘˘˘˘˘˘˘˘˘˘˘˘˘˘˘˘˘˘˘˘˘˘˘˘˘˘˘˘˘˘˘˘˘˘˘˘˘˘
˘˘˘˘˘˘˘˘˘˘˘˘˘˘˘˘˘˘˘˘˘˘˘˘˘˘˘˘˘˘˘˘˘˘˘˘˘˘˘˘˘˘˘˘˘˘˘˘˘˘˘˘˘˘˘˘˘˘˘˘˘˘
˘˘˘˘˘˘˘˘˘˘˘˘˘˘˘˘˘˘˘˘˘˘˘˘˘˘˘˘˘˘˘˘˘˘˘˘¨i•i˘ éø  H jbjb˘˘ $ düdüü˘˘˘˘˘ähhhhhh üÊÊÊÊÜûÂ"
2<P\ ^^^^^^, RVpä h\
\\ä\hh
ü \\\\h
h
\\| ê hhhh\\\\hh\,|"¬Ê\\\µøÂ\…\…\\hûû§B§ûûB   Meeting Agenda:
î Review of last meeting
î Check-ins with team members
î New business
VHûÕ hµÂ hzZhµ ÂÕJPJQJ  )GVH˘˘˘˘˘ gdµÂ H˛  ":pµ Â•-/ "‡=!≈ "≈"≈â†$â†X≈  • ‹ØÕ˘‹Normal CJaJmH    sH   tH   DRØÕ˘°D
   Default Paragraph FontRi ØÕ˘2R Table Normal ^4+
14+  a˘ (kØÕ˘î( No_List 82˘˘Ø8µÂ
Plain Text ÕJQJH ˘˘˘˘ H )ÕVVò ØÂÂ∠ØÊÂò ØÂÂ∠ØÊÂò ØÂÂ∠ØÊÂò ØÂÂ∠ØÊÂòØÂÂ∠ØÊÂ )ÕVVòØ ØÂÂ∠`ù òØ ØÂÂ∠`ù òØ ØÂÂ∠`ù òØpa H  H ˘˘
OLE⊥IñK23
OLE⊥IñK24V UUV˘ØÂ ÂÕ  â û  H˘Ø˘˘  Unknown˘˘˘˘˘˘˘˘˘Õ â    Times New Roman5 ê   ÂSymbol3 ê      Arial3 êNR ø˘Êí  -˘3˘
fg7 ê  Courier  1dé-h 2Âí 2Âí    Î ø•¿WÂÂ 4 Ø Øé•˘˘˘˘˘ ˘˘˘ ˘˘˘ ˘˘˘ ˘˘˘ ˘˘˘ ˘˘˘ ±)÷˘˘  Meeting Agenda:
Mark Hurst
Mark Hurst.˘
   ‡ÕûÕ˘Õh ˘é+'²Õ‹  â ò = ≈ 2 - ‹Î
‹4
Ø L T \ d l ˘ Meeting Agenda: Î ˘John Smithn Î ˘ Normal  John Smithn 1 ˘ Microsoft Word 11.ØØØ‡ \8V« Ø‡ \8V«   Gh ,˘˘˘PICT ^ d ˘
,̆ XX » Î˘Õ MSHD
» î, /Times New Roman /
d.(¥Õ Meetin -˘((¥  g-)2 Â -˘()ag-)2 enda: 3-2˘()ÿ -('Õ• Review of last meetin -˘Ø Q('Îg 2-2 )3  -(ò Õ•
Check(ò )-)î ins with team members 3-2˘ ((ò Î  -(
Õ• New business 3-2˘((
Â 2-2(ÂÕ
ÂÂ˘˘'î»î»ÎîÎî!    «!«ÎîÎî   Â!Â!îÎî   ≈î≈Ê!Ê!   fîfÊ!Ê!   √î√Â!Â!   ¬î¬Ê!Ê!   î!îÂ!Â!   ¿î¿%î%î       ø
!ø•î   ≈•î
ª
!≈fîî
fîî
   ﬞ{!fñî fñî   π!π≈›î ≈›î   ππ‹î‹î  ‹î Σî Σ€î €î   âîâ›î /î ˘+˘,˘
,̆Õ'ú. îò+,˘%Eõ% ˘hpxÂ âèò!
Øf '     Meeting Agenda:  Title     ,˘˘˘
˘˘˘   ˘˘˘   ˘˘˘˘˘˘˘˘˘˘,˘˘˘ ˘˘˘ ˘˘˘˘
˘˘˘˘˘˘˘˘˘˘˘˘˘˘˘˘˘˘˘˘˘˘˘˘˘˘˘˘˘˘˘˘˘˘˘˘˘˘˘˘˘˘˘˘˘˘˘˘˘˘˘˘˘˘˘˘˘˘˘˘˘˘˘˘˘˘˘˘˘˘˘˘˘˘˘˘˘˘˘˘˘˘˘˘˘˘˘˘˘˘Root
Entry ˘˘˘˘˘˘˘˘
¿F ä˘V« $ÂîTable ˘˘˘˘˘˘˘˘˘˘˘˘ WordDocument ˘˘˘˘˘˘˘ SummaryInformation( ˘˘˘˘ DocumentSummaryInformation8 ˘˘˘˘˘˘˘˘˘ CompOb
í             XObjectPool ˘˘˘˘˘˘˘˘  â˘ú  â˘ú«˘˘˘˘˘˘˘˘˘˘˘˘
˘˘˘˘˘˘˘˘˘˘˘˘˘˘˘˘˘˘˘˘˘˘˘˘˘˘˘˘˘˘˘˘˘˘˘˘˘˘˘˘˘˘˘˘˘˘˘˘˘˘˘˘˘˘˘˘˘˘˘˘˘˘˘˘˘˘˘˘˘˘˘˘˘˘˘˘˘˘˘˘˘˘˘˘˘˘
˘˘˘  ˘ ˘  ¿F Microsoft Word Document.˘˘˘MBØH Word.Document.8
```

A Word file contains a *lot* of information. And this is the final difference between Word documents and ASCII documents. While ASCII contains only the characters that the user can see on the screen, Microsoft Word documents can contain the text *and* anything else Microsoft decides to include in the file, without revealing it to the user. Leaving aside all the other disadvantages of Word—the size of the files, the 1980s-era mindset, the expensive succession of upgrades—just the principle here is a problem. It's not a good idea to use a format that hides information in your files without your knowledge or consent. While Word may be unavoidable in some circumstances, users at least need to be aware of how the format works.

British government officials learned this the hard way several years ago. The "dodgy dossier," a Word document containing information that helped justify the government's support of the Iraq war, was sent around to journalists in early 2003. Some enterprising journalist opened the document in a text editor (or had a techie friend do so) and found the names of several unpublished authors of the report. This brought about more controversy, and as the BBC reported in August 2003, "The UK government has now largely abandoned Microsoft Word for documents that become public and has turned to documents created using Adobe Acrobat which uses the Portable Data Format (PDF)."[1] The same article reports that Word files can contain, without the user's knowledge, "the names of document authors, their relationship to each other, earlier versions of documents … [and] occasionally, very personal information such as social security numbers … [and] useful information about the internal network the document travelled through, which could be useful to anyone looking for a route into a network." These are significant risks to run just to create some text.

Text formats: PDF

The article above mentions one other choice for text formats: Adobe's PDF, or Portable Document Format, with the extension .pdf. If a document needs to be created in Word, PDF can contain the data without the accompanying problems of hidden data and incompatibility. In fact *any* application that has a Print command—not just Word—can turn its documents into a PDF.[2] PDF's biggest advantage is shareability: any Mac, Windows, or Linux PC can open and read PDF files without having to buy any

---

1 "The hidden dangers of documents," by Mark Ward, published by the BBC, August 18, 2003. Google the title and you'll find the whole article online, for free. Great piece.

2 On Macs, the Print window of most applications—even Word—has an option to save the document as a PDF. It's more difficult to create PDFs in Windows. Windows users should use one of the many websites that can convert Microsoft documents to PDF, like pdfonline.com or primopdf.com.

special software. Even if the document was created in Word, and the recipient doesn't own Word, the PDF will still be accessible. Moreover, PDF documents look just as good as documents in Word or any other application, both on screen and on paper; there's no degradation of quality. This means that *any* application can create shareable documents, as long as you save the document in PDF. The only drawback of PDF files is that they're read-only, not editable, by recipients. (There are ways of creating editable PDF files, but they require special software.)

Finally, it's worth noting that PDF is a format owned by a corporation—Adobe—which so far hasn't shown any desire to "lock in" or otherwise charge customers for access to the format. (No wonder PDF is so popular.) As long as the recipient doesn't need to edit the file, PDF is a good alternative to Word.

Text formats: final review

Here is a review of which file formats to use when creating digital text:

– If the document doesn't need to be printed, use a text editor to create an ASCII file. If the text needs to be e-mailed, put it in the body of an e-mail—but don't attach it. (Even if the text does need to be printed, ASCII could be an appropriate choice. Since ASCII doesn't include any font or style data, the printed text will look like what comes out of a typewriter, but that might be acceptable. Only if the text needs to look "pretty" on paper should you consider using Word or an equivalent tool.)

– If the document will be printed, and it needs to look "pretty" with formatting and other print-related features, then use Word or an equivalent tool, like Google Docs, to create it. (Advanced users may prefer a professional-grade tool, like Adobe InDesign, for documents that need special formatting or layout.) But share the document in PDF. Only if the recipient needs to edit the file should you share the file in its original (Word) format.

Just remember that Word files may contain hidden data and could be incompatible with any previous version of Word that recipients may be using.

Finally, note that there are other common document formats that are useful to know. Web pages are best created in HTML, databases in FileMaker, spreadsheets in Microsoft Excel or Google Spreadsheet, and slideshows in Apple Keynote or Microsoft PowerPoint. (The "more essentials" chapter revisits these.) For the most part, though, bit-literate users can get through their work with just a Web browser, an e-mail program, and a good text editor. The only other major tool left is the file system.

Chapter 10: **Naming Files**

Whenever the user creates a file—in ASCII, Word, PDF, or any other format—the file needs a name. This goes for any file, whether it's stored somewhere on the user's computer, or attached to an e-mail and sent off. When saving a document, spreadsheet, diagram, or any other file, a window pops up asking the user to name the file. It's an important choice; a good file name makes the file easier to find again later, and it saves time by telling the user what it contains without the user having to open it.

Good file names are especially important when many files are present. For example, if a folder contains twenty files named some variation of "proposal.doc", finding a particular proposal—or a particular revision—can be difficult and time-consuming. A folder with hundreds of files would make the task nearly impossible. Naming files properly helps avoid file overload and makes users much more productive.

Unfortunately, many users choose ineffective file names because they never learned how to name files properly. Here are some common "worst practices":

- Non-descriptive file names, like "agenda.doc" and "notes.doc", which could refer to many different projects or contexts. As stated above, such file names are even more problematic when multiple files are present with similar names.

- File names including the word "final", as in "final report.doc". There's no better way to guarantee that you'll need a revision than to name something "final". Inevitably, the following versions become "final report revised.doc" and "final report revised USE THIS VERSION.doc". It's difficult to find the right one later.

– File names including the word "new". Even if the file is more recent than the last version, what happens when there are future revisions? The name "new new new report.doc" is hardly effective.

– Resumes named "resume.doc". As an employer, I can attest to the frequency with which applicants name their resumes this, which makes all the resume files look the same as they arrive. It's impossible to sort through them unless I go through and manually rename them properly. (Because of this, my company has a policy of only accepting job applications without attachments. The resume has to be pasted in the body of an e-mail. Problem solved.)

These problems are all avoided by following a simple bit-literate file naming scheme. A good file name contains just enough information about the file to describe what's inside, and omits everything else. Each part of a file name should contain useful information, or "any difference that makes a difference."* The only catch is that users have to be consistent in naming files with this scheme, or the system will break down. As with every other part of bit literacy, only after sustained practice does it begin to pay off.

The naming scheme

A bit-literate file name should contain the following fields, separated by hyphens: initials of the person who created the file, creation date, and topic or keyword. An extension may optionally be added. Shown as a template, the naming scheme looks like this:

initials-date-topic.extension

---

* This was anthropologist Gregory Bateson's definition of "information," from his 1979 book *Mind and Nature*.

For example, for my draft of the book written on September 25 and saved as an ASCII file, the name might look like this:

mh-0925-bookdraft.txt

Correspondingly, a file named js-0313-projectplan.pdf could be John Smith's project plan from March 13.

This one scheme can create a bit-literate name for all kinds of files:

- files you create (a letter to Aunt Marge, notes from a meeting, a sketch of a new design)

- files you save (a receipt you download from a website, or any e-mail you receive)

- or any other files you need to name.

In each case, the file name shows who created the bits, when, and for what purpose. The file name thus represents the file as a "snapshot" of bits at one moment. This has practical consequences for how users work with files: users should save successive revisions to a file in separate files, with separate file names. This helps guard against data being inadvertently lost.

Each component of the file name is explained in detail below.

Author initials

The file name starts by showing the user, without opening the file, who created the bits. The file name should usually contain the author's initials, not the full name, since it's quicker to type only two characters. (It's important to fill out every part of the file name with the least amount of typing.) Two characters is the minimum to identify someone, though of course there can be cases—when two users' initials are identical, for example—when it's better to use the author's first or full name.

It's occasionally helpful to make exceptions to the naming scheme. For example, if a folder contains a bunch of files that I've created, and I'm the only person accessing the folder, then typing "mh" at the beginning of every file name would be redundant. In this case, for files I've created I replace the author field with either "notes" (if I'm taking notes on a meeting, call, or just have ideas to write at a certain moment), or for an e-mail or file that I've sent to someone else, I type "to" and the *recipient's* initials.

For example:

notes-0923-callwpt.txt would be notes I took during a call on September 23 with PT.

to-js-0925-comments.txt would contain comments (perhaps an e-mail) that I sent to JS on September 25.

Still, it's best to use the naming scheme consistently at first, before exploring exceptions.

Hyphen

Sitting between the author initials and the date is a hyphen. It's important to use the hyphen—and no other character, like a slash or a space—to separate the parts of the file name. This is because the hyphen is one of the few separators that all major platforms—Macintosh, Windows, Linux, and the Web—can accept in file names without trouble.* Another character that works across all platforms is the underscore character, the "_". But that's harder to type, since it requires holding down the Shift key. The hyphen is easier to type, so it's the better choice.

---

* If the file might be uploaded to the Web, it's especially important to avoid the space character. On the Web, any space in a file name turns into "%20". For example, if a file was named "mh 0925 notes.htm" and posted online, Web browsers would show the file name as "mh%200925%20notes.htm". Better to use hyphens.

Creation date

The date field contains only four digits—two for the month, and two for the day—in "mmdd" format. This raises several possible questions: Why not include the year? What about the European "ddmm" format, with the day coming before the month? Wouldn't it be more accurate, and sortable, to put the date in year-month-day format? All of these are valid questions, and the short answer is that users should use whatever format is most convenient for them and the people they share files with. The important thing is to include the date in *some* consistent format. (Some files don't need a date at all in their file names, as discussed later.)

There is, however, a reason why the year doesn't show up in the naming scheme: it's usually not needed. Most projects don't last more than a year and so the month and day are sufficient. It's also faster and easier to type the file name without the year digits. (For longer projects, files should be archived in year-folders, as described in the next chapter.)

Incidentally, typing the date doesn't have to be a chore. A bit lever like Typinator, Typeit4me, or ActiveWords can type the current date on command. (Bit levers are covered in the "other essentials" chapter.)

Finally, it's important to use two digits for the month—e.g., "01" for January, not "1". This is so that when the files are sorted by name, all the files authored by the same person will also be sorted by date. For example, the files below are sorted alphabetically:

> mh-0103-notes.txt
> mh-0512-coverdraft.pdf
> mh-1122-revision.pdf
> pt-0122-comments.txt
> pt-0513-comments.txt
> pt-1123-callnotes.txt

All of the files are grouped by author, and because the dates all have four digits, within each group the files are sorted chronologically.

(If the January 22 file had a date of "122" instead of "0122", it wouldn't be sorted correctly.)

Topic

The topic, like the author initials and date, lets the user know what's in the file without having to open it. For example, the topic of the file mh-0512-bookdraft.txt tells me that this is a draft of the book. Looking at a set of files with topics, it's easy to spot the call notes, book drafts, and contracts, just by reading the file names. Topics can be separated-by-hyphens or MashedUpTogether, depending on each user's preference.

Unlike the author initials and date, the topic is optional. While the topic is usually helpful, some files are unimportant enough that they're not worth the user's effort to type in a topic. For example, saving an ordinary e-mail from John Smith, I might just call it js-0925.txt, and if he sends several during the day I would just use digits to designate the order: js-0925-1.txt, js-0925-2.txt, and so on.

Extension

Most Windows software adds the file extension (e.g., ".txt" or ".pdf" in the example files above) automatically when creating a file, so users don't have to type it. And on Macs, the extension is usually unnecessary if the file is going to be used only on Macs. However, Mac users who might share a file with Windows users may need to manually add the extension, since Windows often needs the extension in order to know what application to open it with.*

---

* Mac users need to know these extensions: .doc for Word files, .ppt for PowerPoint files, .xls for Excel files, .txt for plaintext files, .pdf for PDF files, and .htm or .html for Web-friendly HTML files. I don't understand why a twenty-first century operating system should need file extensions, invented for computers in the 1960s, but so it is.

Space name files

While the file naming scheme is usually helpful, there are some special kinds of files that are worth making exceptions for. One is the "space name" file.

In a given folder there are often one or two files that you open much more frequently than any others. The trick is to name these popular files with a space character at the beginning, so that they are listed first—at the very top of the project folder—when files are sorted by name.[1] This makes it easier and quicker to access those files. When viewing any folder, just hitting the space bar usually selects the top file, allowing you to then open it with a single keystroke.

For example, in my project folders, I often create a file called " contact" (that's the space character, then the word "contact", without the quotation marks) to hold the contact information of everyone involved in the project. Without this special file, their contact info might be scattered across different locations—in an address book, a shared database, or on a website somewhere. The " contact" file makes things easier, since whenever I need to find someone's e-mail, phone number, or postal address, I know exactly where to look. Moreover, the amount of data in the file is limited, since it's confined to the people on that project. Instead of searching Outlook or some other address book and scrolling through an endless list of names, I can open " contact" and find the person right away.[2]

There are many possible uses of this trick, like a " schedule" file, if the project schedule is something you often need to consult. Just

---

1 Windows and Linux users may find it better to use an underscore instead of a space character.

2 Address book tools can be problematic. The file formats tend to be proprietary, the user interfaces are poor, and the data is hard to share with people who aren't using the same software. An ASCII " contacts" file solves all of these problems. If you need to manage or share hundreds of contacts or more, FileMaker—easy database software available at www.filemaker.com—is a good choice.

remember that space name files work only if they're exceptions and not the rule. The fewer such files there are in a project folder, the more prominent they are.

Ongoing files: canvases and log files

The distinctive quality of space name files, apart from their name, is that the user edits them on an ongoing basis. This is precisely why they *don't* contain a date in the file name. In contrast, a file named using the naming scheme includes the creation date, since it is a "one-off" or snapshot of bits created at one moment, on one day.

There are two kinds of ongoing files: the canvas and the log file. (All space name files are ongoing, though not all ongoing file names need to start with a space.)

A canvas is any file that the user may want to continually edit, making changes and saving them in the same file. A canvas's file name doesn't include a date, since the canvas may contain bits from many different days. For example, the " contact" file described above is a canvas, since the user can continually update the file to keep everyone's contact information up to date.

A specialized type of canvas is the log file. This is a canvas divided into individual entries that are organized chronologically, much like a diary. Generally the most recent entry is on top, so that the user can add new data, and see recent entries, without scrolling down. Older entries continue beneath. The dividers between entries can be the dates themselves. For example, a log file called "book progress" might include the following text:

```
02/15/07
revised chapter 9
added layout notes
02/14/07
revised chapter 8
verified quote in Wikipedia
```

Here are some of the log files I maintain on my computer:

- "movies i've watched": I've kept up this log file for years. It lists every movie I've seen since I started the file, and a one-line review of each. The dividers in this file aren't days, as in the example above, but years: the current year's movies are at the top of the list, followed by last year's, then the year's before that, and so on. I also maintain a similar file called "books i've read".

- "health": This is a log file in which I record any illness or medical condition my wife or I have had, and the date range of the symptoms. It's easy to review later how many times we were out sick, how long things lasted, or what the doctor advised. Many people keep diligent records about the maintenance history of their cars; I think a personal health log is even more important. It also doesn't require any special tool, just a text editor to create the ASCII file. (Soon enough the technology industry will sell many products promising to solve this need—EasyFamilyHealthLog.com or some such. Not only will these products be unnecessary for bit-literate users, they could be risky. Users should be wary of allowing companies to mediate access to their own health information. This is one bitstream users should have complete control over.)

Canvases and log files can be helpful in many ways, but they come with an important caveat: they're more susceptible to loss. Since the user always updates the same file when making edits, past versions of the file aren't automatically stored. This is unlike normal "one-off" files, which naturally result in a trail of past versions to refer to if something goes wrong. (For example, a series of report drafts will all be stored in the project folder as different files, possibly with different dates in their file names.) One errant edit in a canvas or log file, though, can change or delete a lot of data in that one file. Thus it's important to make frequent backups of your most important canvas and log files.*

Final thoughts on file naming

Some users may wonder why they should bother with any naming scheme, since the computer's file system attaches its own metadata to every file. For example, the computer stores, and displays, the date and time that each file was most recently modified. This data may occasionally be helpful, but it's unreliable. Sometimes just opening a file to view its contents can change the modification date, even if no changes were actually made. And if the file system crashes, restoring the files from a backup can change the modification date of all the files. Using the naming scheme, though, ensures that the author initials, creation date, and topic will remain in the file name.

The bit-literate user should never depend on a file system, application, or any other tool to operate properly, and instead should stay focused on the bits themselves. The user's bits, after all, are the most supremely important thing on the entire computer. The hardware can die, the software can become out of date—*anything* can happen, but as long as the user's files are named right, organized well, and backed up, there's nothing to worry about. The file naming scheme "bakes in" good data to each file name, guaranteeing that the files will be usable and effective no matter where the user takes them. Bit literacy liberates users from being locked into any particular software or hardware. Combined with the storage scheme described in the next chapter, good file names allow the user to confidently say, "Have bits, will travel."

---

* Backup is covered more in the "other essentials" chapter, but an easy way to back up a single file is to e-mail it to a free e-mail account at Yahoo Mail or Gmail. Put the name of the file and today's date in the Subject line, attach the file to the message, and send it. For example, the Subject line could be "movies i've watched 02-25-07", and the file itself, "movies i've watched", would be attached to the otherwise blank e-mail.

Chapter 11: **Storing Files**

Different kinds of files are best organized in different ways. Photos, for example, are best managed within an application dedicated to photos, like iPhoto or Picasa, using the method described in the photos chapter. Music is best organized in a program like iTunes. But that's not the case with all files. Often we create or receive bits that don't have the advantage of a dedicated application.

Suppose you type a personal letter, print it out, and postal-mail it to Aunt Marge, but you still want to hold on to the original file. The first step, of course, is to give it a bit-literate file name. But that's not enough, since you still need to store the file on the computer so that you can find it again later. There's no "iLetter" application that organizes personal letters. The file has to live somewhere; there must be some catch-all place to store files that aren't managed by another application.

There is such a catch-all: the *file system,* the application that stores and organizes all types of files. Every computer has one—Mac, Windows, and Linux—and some Web applications offer "online file systems" that allow users to store and organize files online. Even applications like iPhoto and iTunes use the computer's file system, behind the scenes, to organize the user's files; they just show the files in a prettier format than the file system would. It's like getting laundry done at a luxury hotel. The hotel uses the same washing machines and detergent that you might use at home, but the hotel staff hand-delivers the clothes, nicely folded.

While some types of files get the "luxury treatment" from iPhoto and iTunes, others only have the file system. This isn't a problem. For bit-literate users, the file system offers an elegant and efficient way of organizing all kinds of files. Users just need to know how it works.

First, a quick tour. When you turn on your computer, the first thing that shows up is the desktop, which displays the hard drive icon (or "My Computer" in Windows) and the icons of any files that have been placed on the desktop. Double-clicking the hard drive displays the top of the file system's hierarchy: folders here contain other folders, which contain yet other folders, and on down through many levels. Any folder can contain any number of files or folders. Thus any file on the computer—the letter to Aunt Marge, any photo, any song, or other kind of file—ultimately lives somewhere, in some folder, within the hierarchy of the file system. (Files on the desktop are within the file system, too.)

Unfortunately, most users have never learned how to use the file system effectively, so they are unsure of what folders to create or how to organize files within them. Here are some common pitfalls:

- Some people create *too many* folders, resulting in a jumbled mess, or an impossibly deep hierarchy, and thus can't find files later—or even decide where to store new files.

- Others create *too few* folders, dumping everything into one or two places, and thus can't find files later because of the clutter.

- Sometimes people dump everything onto the desktop, cramming it with icons—a demoralizing sight whenever it's visible.

- Worse of all, some users are *partially* organized. They follow one method for awhile, then dump things randomly for awhile, then try something else for awhile. As a result, their file system is a crazy quilt of abandoned organizational schemes, and they are utterly at a loss whenever they have to store or find a file, because they don't know which scheme to follow.

Seeing that many users don't want to organize their own files, the technology industry offers its own solutions—at a price. The tools promise to help users find their files later without requiring the pesky discipline of getting organized. Users presumably can dump files anywhere—making a mess of the file system, or cramming every file they have onto the desktop—and the tool will find any file with a simple search query. The reality, however, is not so pretty. The more files a user has, the less likely the search will come up with the right result. And searching is just one activity: users may more often want to browse a set of files having to do with a certain topic. This is much more easily accomplished with the file system.

The file system is also valuable because it allows users direct access to their files, with minimal distractions from tools or companies that may want to mediate that access. The bit-literate filing scheme described below gives you full control over how your bits are stored and organized. All file systems work in more or less the same way, so if you ever have to switch machines or operating systems, your bits will be organized in a way that transfers anywhere. With bit literacy, in other words, you're free. Free to choose whatever is the best technology at any one moment, free to work effectively and efficiently with bits of all kinds at all times, and free from the constraints of any operating system, application, or technology company.

But there's a cost. Organizing files properly requires a small amount of discipline, though only the smallest possible amount to get the job done. Here, as in other areas, bit literacy follows Occam's razor: things should go as far as they need to, but no further.* In fact, most files can fit within a simple two-level storage system, not unlike what's described in the "managing photos" chapter. It's easy to set up.

The parent folder

First, identify (or create) the "parent folder" that will serve as the top level of the storage hierarchy. (This will contain all of your files that are not already handled by another tool like iPhoto, iTunes,

---

* According to Wikipedia, the original quote from William of Ockham is "entities should not be multiplied beyond necessity." That's practically the definition of bit-literate file management.

or the e-mail program.) Depending on the operating system, your personal preferences, and—if you're in an office environment—the policies of the IT team, there are many different ways to create or identify the parent folder. In Windows, the My Documents folder is a good choice. On a Mac, the user's Home folder or Documents folder can serve as the parent folder. (Some Mac users may prefer to put the parent folder on the top level of the hard drive, available by double-clicking the hard drive icon on the desktop.) You may also want to maintain a separate parent folder for personal files; we'll return to that idea, but for now we'll focus on the parent folder, which contains all work-related files.

Inside the parent folder are two levels of storage. Here's what the hierarchy looks like:

— Parent folder

  – Level 1: Project folders and category folders (described in detail below), but *no* files

    – Level 2: Properly named files and optional sub-folders (also described below)

For example, a parent folder named Documents might look like this:

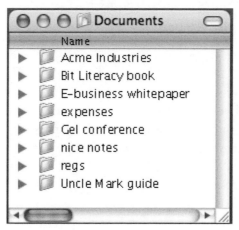

The parent folder should contain folders only, no files. Each folder should have a simple and descriptive name referring to a project or general file category.

The project folder

Each project folder should be named after a client ("Acme Industries") or a general project ("Bit Literacy book") and should contain properly named files related to that project. It may also contain some sub-folders. For example, the Acme Industries project folder might look like this:

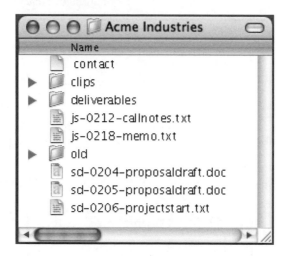

When creating a project folder, the user must decide whether it will be *a* place to store files related to the project, or the *only* place. This usually means deciding where to store project-related e-mails, often the most important bitstream in a project. Should they stay in the e-mail program itself, or should the user save them to the project folder in the file system? (Saving e-mails to the file system is easy: in most e-mail programs there is a "Save As" option under the File menu, which saves the e-mail as an ASCII (.txt) file. The user just needs to name the file properly and navigate to the correct project folder before clicking Save.*)

Whether for short-term convenience or because of a lack of training, many users keep all their project e-mails in the e-mail program, either in an e-mail folder or (unfortunately) piled up in the inbox. This can create problems. The bits are susceptible to loss if the e-mail program crashes, and until then they're "locked in": it's harder to take the bits with you if you ever want to change e-mail programs. While there usually exists some way to export e-mails into competing e-mail programs, technology companies don't make it easy, for obvious reasons.

The biggest problem with storing project e-mails in the e-mail program is that it makes project files harder to find, since they'll then reside in multiple places. The e-mail program can't store *all* the files for a project, after all. Setting aside the possibility of photos or audio, consider the variety of documents that a project can generate:

— Incoming e-mails (communications from team members or people associated with the project)

— Outgoing e-mails (messages that the user writes and sends to other team members, the boss, or the client)

— Meeting notes that the user writes (using a text editor or Word) and saves onto the hard drive

— Meeting notes that another team member writes and then e-mails as an attachment

— Drafts of deliverable documents—contracts, spreadsheets, presentations, and so on—and successive revisions

— Finalized, approved, and delivered versions of those documents

---

* As described in the "more essentials" chapter, a tool like Default Folder (for the Mac) or FileBox eXtender (for Windows) can make folder navigation much easier. Used with a program like QuicKeys to assign a keystroke to the Save As command, and a bit lever to type the date in the file name, it can be faster to file e-mails in the file system than in the e-mail program.

To manage these bitstreams, most users unfortunately do what's easiest in the short term: they let the bits stay wherever they were originally created. This is "organizing by default," the worst possible strategy, and it leaves users disorganized, out of control, and thus susceptible to any technology company that promises to fix the mess. Consider what happens when files sit where they arrive, or wherever they go by default when the user clicks "Save":

- Incoming e-mails stay in the e-mail inbox—along with all other kinds of incoming e-mail, project-related or not.

- Outgoing e-mails stay in the Sent Mail folder—along with every other e-mail the user sends, project-related or not.

- Meeting notes stay wherever Microsoft Word happens to put the file when the user clicks Save—typically the desktop or a messy Documents folder, where a random assortment of non-project-related files may reside.

- Deliverable documents—drafts, revisions, and final versions—could sit in any number of places, depending on what software created them. The bits could be in the user's e-mail program as an attachment, on the user's desktop, in a generic Documents folder, or in a shared environment used by a project team: an intranet, extranet, or a Web-based workspace.

Organizing by default scatters project files to many different locations, which makes it difficult and time-consuming for anyone to find a given file. If someone asks, "Where is that last version of the PowerPoint file that we were working on last week?", team members may have to check their inboxes, e-mail folders, desktops, and the intranet, just to cover the first few possible locations. Worse yet, they may then have to compare files to see who found the right revision. Without consistently following a discipline for storage, the file could be anywhere, named anything, and found alongside any number of irrelevant files.

In contrast, storing files in a project folder, in the file system, makes it quick and easy to find files. It's like the fail-safe method of never losing one's keys at home: just put them in the same place, every time, when you get home. If an item belongs in only one place, and the user always puts it there, then there's never a question of where to find it later. The goal of bit-literate file management, then, is to *minimize the possible locations for a given file,* ideally storing all files related to a project in a single folder.

Given different technology environments, and the various demands on a user or project team, the goal of "one folder" is sometimes unachievable. Project teams, for example, may require individual members to store some files on their own computers, while sharing other files in a team workspace. Even so, the goal remains to *minimize* the potential locations for a file. Especially for an individual user, the ideal of one folder is often achievable.

To sum up, there are two main advantages to this approach:

— It's easier to find a given project file, since there's only one folder in the file system where it could be. There's no need to search the entire computer. And once the user opens the project folder, the bit-literate file names make it much easier to find the desired file.

— Files stored in the file system are easily transferable. This is in contrast to e-mails stored in an e-mail program, which are "locked in" to that application only. Files in the file system can move freely. They're easy to back up, share with friends or coworkers, or move to a different computer—even a different operating system.*

One other way to minimize the possible locations for a file is to avoid using sub-folders.

---

* Two invaluable tools in transferring files: software, like ZipIt, that creates a compressed "zip" archive of multiple files; and a USB flash drive to physically carry the bits into another device. Ask a techie friend to show you these tools, if you're not sure.

About sub-folders

Sub-folders that sit inside the project folder should be avoided except in certain situations. This may be a difficult guideline for users who like to over-organize their folders into sub-folders, sub-sub-folders inside them, and so on—but there's little value in having so many levels in the storage hierarchy. The goal of bit literacy is to *minimize* the time you spend getting organized, so as to *maximize* your time for more important things, like working efficiently and enjoying life outside work. Sub-folders generally don't improve on the bit-literate system of properly named files, all sitting together in a single project folder.

There are exceptions, however. A sub-folder or two can optionally serve for specialized uses. For example, a project folder may contain one or more of the following sub-folders:

- An "old" folder, for files so old that they are no longer relevant but still need to be archived. In a long project spanning several years, the "old" folder can be replaced with "year folders"— "2005", "2006", etc.—containing project files from those calendar years. (This also saves the user from typing the year into the date field of file names, since the containing folder would show if they're from a past year.)

- A "deliverables" folder to hold the documents that were delivered and accepted by the client (or boss or other recipient). The file names don't have to include the word "final", since residing in the "deliverables" folder implies that these are the release versions of the files. Having such a folder makes it much easier to retrieve the milestone documents for a project without a bunch of irrelevant drafts cluttering the folder. One iron-clad rule, though, is that users can put a file in the "deliverables" folder only *after* the client confirms that they accept the file as the deliverable.

- A "clips" folder containing press clippings about the project: either mentioning the client by name, or touching on a topic related to the project and thus useful for later reference. In this case, the "clips" folder then operates as a category folder, containing a bitstream of one particular type, and thus can use a more relaxed naming scheme. Category folders are described below.

The category folder

Unlike a project folder, which holds many different types of files pertaining to one project, a category folder contains one *kind* of file. While occasionally a category folder may sit inside a project folder (as in the example of "clips" above), most category folders sit on the first level of the parent folder, alongside all other project folders.

Here are some other common examples of category folders:

– "expenses": This folder stores past expense reports and digital receipts. These should be dated with the standard file naming scheme, since the file might be shared with other users or an accounting department. (For example, "mh-011607-expenses.xls" would be an Excel spreadsheet showing my expense report from January 16, 2007.) An "old" or "already handled" sub-folder is good to set up, too, to hold past expense reports and receipts that have been taken care of. This reduces clutter by separating out past, irrelevant documents that simply need to be archived. An "expenses" folder may look like this:

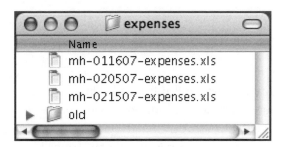

– "regs": This folder can contain all the passwords, registrations, and welcome e-mails from websites you register for. The files in this folder are created either by saving an e-mail (e.g., a confirmation e-mail from a website you signed up with) or by creating a text file and typing in the username and password yourself. Either way, the file naming scheme is easy: just name each file after the website or application it pertains to. For example, a file in the "regs" folder called "nytimes" would contain your username and password for the nytimes.com website. A file called "Microsoft Office" would contain the registration code for your copy of Microsoft Office. The "regs" folder solves the problem of lost registrations; all of your data is in the right folder, clearly named, and thus easy to find.

– "nice notes": This is the place to store any especially nice or gratifying e-mails you've received from colleagues over the years. Don't let these important messages get lost in the shuffle; instead, give them a permanent home here. Name them however you like, but use the file naming scheme if you intend to scan for particular messages later.

Unless the files in a category folder are likely to be shared (like those in the "expenses" folder), they generally don't need to follow a strict naming scheme. Files in category folders are more homogeneous than files in project folders, so it doesn't take much to distinguish between them. For example, in a "regs" folder, each file should simply be named after the website in question; using the full file naming scheme wouldn't add useful information.

The Personal folder

One last folder to consider creating is a *second* parent folder, separate from the first, called Personal. This can be a useful folder on computers that are used for both work and personal reasons; those two sets of files are best stored separately. The Personal folder can then operate as an informal scrapbook of any files that the user considers personally meaningful: letters, e-mails, or anything else.

Several category folders may be helpful in the Personal folder:

- "info" or "important": This can be a general folder for storing important information like health account data or a text file containing contact information of friends and family. File names here should be short and descriptive—"health insurance" or "addresses", for example.

- "clips": A folder for personally interesting news clippings, saved in bit-literate clip format. (Year sub-folders can archive past years' clips.)

- "writing": An archive of any personal writing—notes, letters, drafts, or other scribblings.

- "taxes [year]" (e.g., "taxes 2007"): A folder storing all notes, e-mails, and digital receipts pertaining to that tax year. Every January I create a new "taxes" folder to hold all tax-related receipts and notes I get throughout the year, so that I'll be fully organized for the next year's tax filing.

- A year folder, like "2006": a scrapbook of miscellaneous items from a past year. I create a new year folder at the end of each year, so my Personal folder contains several year folders.

Finally, note that unlike the main, work-related parent folder, Personal can contain files as well as folders on its first level. Except for folders like those described above, Personal can mainly serve as a repository of any interesting files. A little clutter is OK here, since it's separated from the main parent folder and won't affect the user's efficiency at work.

Managing the desktop

Outside the one or two parent folders, there's only one other place in the file system that the user needs to keep organized: the desktop. This is often the most misused location in the entire file system. As noted above, organizing by default allows files to lie where they're created, and that often sends them to the desktop. A cluttered desktop is especially conspicuous—to the user, and even to coworkers passing by. It's usually visible below any open applications, and it always appears during startup. So just like an empty inbox and an empty todo list, it's important for the sake of your productivity—and morale—to keep the desktop empty of all unnecessary icons and files.

An empty desktop also has the benefit of making the occasional visiting file that much more prominent. Files on the desktop are like sticky notes on the monitor: one item stands out nicely, reminding the user to give it attention, but more than that quickly turn into distracting clutter. So the desktop can be an effective place to store a few files *temporarily*, in order to draw the user's attention to them, but that should be the exception. As a rule, keep the desktop empty.

Induction: organizing the file system for the first time

Some users may find it difficult to set up the parent, project, and category folders described above, since their files are already disorganized. This calls for induction—organizing the file system for the first time—using a process similar to the inbox-induction method described in the "managing incoming e-mail" chapter.

These are the steps for file system induction:

— Identify or create a parent folder, if one isn't present already.

— Create an "old" folder inside the parent folder. Include the current date, including the year, in the name. For example, if induction takes place on December 1, 2007, name the folder "old-120107".

— Find all project-related files and folders, wherever they sit in the file system, and drag them into the "old" folder. The parent folder should still be empty except for the "old" folder, which should contain *all* project-related files and folders in the file system. Thus the desktop should be empty, too. (If the e-mail program contains project-related e-mails, it's the user's choice whether to save them into the file system, too.) The "old" folder may be a real mess at this point, but that's OK.

- In the parent folder, create (empty) folders for all appropriate projects and categories. Create sub-folders inside those folders only if they're necessary.

- Open the "old" folder and drag any vitally important files into the project and category folders where they belong. Immediately rename those files with bit-literate file names. The majority of files may stay in the "old" folder, though. (It's no worse than having them scattered across the file system, and it might take too much time to organize each and every file.) Later on you can always move more files from "old" into the right project folder, as you encounter them.

Once induction is complete, the file system is organized and ready to accept new files. The parent folder contains the right project and category folders, which in turn hold properly named files. The "old" folder guarantees that nothing was lost in the process, and the date in the folder name marks when the user took control of the file system and began working more productively.

Chapter 12: **Other Essentials**

The following are some other tools, skills, and guidelines that the bit-literate practitioner must know.

Touch typing

It's easy to get excited about technology—the tools, the features, and all the possibilities they offer—and forget about the simplest, most basic things that help us the most. Typing is perhaps the best example of this. There are no celebrity typists, no magazine cover stories on typing, and no talks on typing at high-tech conferences. Yet many occupations today require typing—a *lot* of typing—all the time, all day, in nearly all applications. Typing speed can be one of the best predictors of a user's overall productivity. For this reason my company gives a typing test to every potential hire, and we take it seriously if a candidate can't touch type.

The keyboard is supremely important to bit-literate users because it's their primary input device. The mouse, and everything it clicks, like hyperlinks and application icons, are all secondary; users must primarily know how to use the keyboard. And that means touch typing. It's unacceptable for someone to have to look at the keyboard to remember where the keys are, or to use only 20% of one's fingers—the "hunt and peck" method with two forefingers—when eight other perfectly healthy fingers are available. You might as well drive a sports car only in first gear because you've never bothered to learn how to change gears correctly. For physically able users, there is absolutely no excuse for not knowing how to touch type.

Sixty words per minute is a good baseline speed to achieve—using all ten fingers and without looking at the keys. With concentrated practice, and the use of a bit lever (described below), it's not difficult to exceed one hundred words per minute.*

I'll never forget an experience I once had at an "emerging technology" conference. A very smart programmer was excitedly demonstrating his new software, which allowed users to fly through hundreds of bitstreams—pictures, e-mails, calendars, and on and on—in the slickest way possible. Throughout the demo he stood there, this very nice and smart guy, pecking out each—letter—on—the—keyboard—with—one—single—finger. I thought to myself, this guy just spent a year of his life creating a tool that may or may not help people fly around information more quickly—and yet he could have *doubled* his productivity by just learning how to type. "Learn to type!" I wanted to tell him. But the law of techie conferences is to acknowledge the cool features and otherwise stay quiet, so I didn't say anything.

This is a non-negotiable point worth restating. To become bit-literate, you must know how to touch type. So *learn to type.*

For advanced users: typing in Dvorak

Since the keyboard is the primary input device, it makes sense that bit-literate users should learn to use it efficiently. But this can mean more than touch typing. Although it requires a sizable investment of time, the advanced bit-literate user should consider learning the best possible keyboard technology.

Years ago when I began my career as a user-experience consultant, I took stock of how I worked on the computer to make sure that I "walked the talk." To be a legitimate user advocate, asking people and companies to change their ways, I felt that I needed to commit to using only the most efficient tools, interfaces, and methods.

---

* It's even faster to type in all lower-case letters, since it avoids having to reach for the Shift key. I often type in all lower-case unless it's an official or formal context, when I'll buckle down and use the Shift key—much like dressing up for an important meeting.

Almost immediately I found an embarrassingly obvious gap in my portfolio. The interface I used the most—the keyboard—was all wrong. Its arrangement of keys, or keymap, was horribly designed, even user-hostile. This was the "Qwerty" keymap, named after the letters on the top row of keys, found on keyboards and typewriters everywhere.

Qwerty was designed in the age of mechanical typewriters, when typing too quickly resulted in jamming the mechanical rods together.[1] To avoid jams, Qwerty was designed with common keys and key combinations placed in hard-to-reach spots, in order to slow typists down. The Qwerty standard endured, and today hundreds of millions of people use an interface that places needless strain on their wrists and fingers. Unsurprisingly, Qwerty can cause RSI—repetitive stress injury—in users who type for long periods. RSI is a debilitating condition that can require surgery and months of recuperation, with no typing allowed, sometimes without a full recovery.

I know about Qwerty and RSI from personal experience. Early in my career, my wrists were often in pain after sustained typing. This was just after college, where I'm sure I did permanent harm to my wrists in the MIT computer labs, typing for hours at a time. As I considered the problem—and the potential hypocrisy—of working as a user advocate while using this poorly designed keymap, I found a solution that gave me healthier wrists, higher productivity, and a clear conscience.

The solution was the Dvorak keymap, an alternate arrangement of keys on the standard keyboard that makes typing easier, faster, and more accurate.[2] I switched permanently to Dvorak, and after a month of practice, I was back to comfortable touch-typing. I soon

---

1 Wikipedia credits Christopher Sholes, a Milwaukee newspaper editor, for designing Qwerty in the 1860s, patenting it in 1868, and selling it to Remington in 1873.

2 Wikipedia credits Dr. August Dvorak, a University of Washington professor, and William Dealey with inventing Dvorak in the 1930s. Some studies dispute the increase in speed from using Dvorak, but I've lived it.

surpassed my previous typing rate, which was already fast, and I've never had wrist trouble since.

It's easy to switch a keyboard from Qwerty to Dvorak by enabling the right setting in the operating system. (Mac, Windows, and Linux all have this capability.) Having done so, the user can type normally on the regular keyboard, with the keys yielding different characters than they did previously. For example, in Qwerty, the letter under the right middle finger is K. In Dvorak, pressing that same key yields a T. Seeing that T is a more common letter than K gives an idea of why Dvorak is so effective. The Dvorak keymap arranges keys by prevalence, placing common letters and combinations of letters where they're easier to type. Many common words—"the", "that", "not", "she", and others—can be typed in Dvorak without moving the fingers from their home positions.

This is the Dvorak keyboard layout:*

The all-important middle row is where the fingers can type, quickly and comfortably, without having to reach to another row. Qwerty's middle row is a train wreck: ASDGF on the left hand, HJKL;' on the right hand. Compare that to Dvorak: AOEUI on the left, DHTNS- on the right. Dvorak's middle row contains all the most popular letters in English, with vowels on the left hand and consonants on the right.

Typing in Dvorak is faster, easier, more accurate, and physically healthier—all aims of bit literacy. What's more, the Dvorak

* Image from the Wikipedia page for the Dvorak Simplified Keyboard:
  http://en.wikipedia.org/wiki/Dvorak_Simplified_Keyboard

keymap itself is free, not copyrighted or owned by any company, and it's available instantly. Like all other parts of bit literacy, it just requires consistent practice for the user to reap tremendous long-term benefits.

The bit lever

Archimedes, the ancient Greek mathematician and philosopher, famously said that with a long enough lever and a place to stand, he could move the earth. The idea is similarly powerful in the bit world. Properly set up, a piece of software known as a *bit lever* can take small inputs and generate huge outputs. Knowing how to use a bit lever is essential to bit literacy.

A bit lever can dramatically increase a user's typing speed by automatically typing common words or phrases. For example, many users must repeatedly type the name of their organization in e-mails, documents, and Web forms. But there's no reason for the user's fingers to type the whole thing every time. Repetitive tasks like this are the computer's job, not the user's. The user should not have to type *anything* that the computer knows already or can learn easily enough: the user's name or organization, the current date, common phrases, stock answers, and other common text. So even though touch-typing is essential, an even better way to create text is to have the computer type it for you.

This is how a bit lever works: whenever you type an abbreviation and then hit a trigger, like the space bar, the abbreviation instantly gets replaced with an expansion that you've defined previously. For example, on my computer if I type "cg" and hit the space bar, "cg" instantly turns into "Creative Good". The abbreviation-expansion function is all a bit lever does, but that one function holds tremendous value for bit-literate users.

Here are just a few uses of a bit lever:

- *Correcting misspellings:* "teh" becomes "the", and "taht" becomes "that". This allows users to type much faster, since common misspellings are corrected on the fly. It's fun to blaze away on the keyboard and watch in amusement as the bit lever fixes misspellings in the cursor's wake. (Even though typing in Dvorak is more accurate than Qwerty, I still get plenty of use from this function.)

– *Typing long words or phrases:* I use the word "experience" a lot, but using my bit lever I just type "ex". Similarly, "ce" becomes "customer experience", "env" becomes "environment", and so on. Common phrases work, too: "tf" becomes "thanks for"; "tfy" becomes "thanks for your"; "tvmfy" becomes "thanks very much for your"; and so on. A bit lever can make you more efficient and more polite at the same time.

– *Typing entire messages:* This is especially useful for custom responses in e-mail—for answers to common questions, customer service responses, and the like. I simply define the abbreviation and expansion once, and it's available from then on.

– *Typing long URLs:* It's easy to point people to my various websites as I write e-mails. "geu" turns into http://goodexperience.com, "cgu" leads to http://creativegood.com, and "blu" turns into http://bitliteracy.com. I can also point to a specific page: for my Gel 2007 conference, for example, I just type "g7u" and it types the URL: http://gelconference.com/c/gel07.php

– *Managing passwords:* My wsj.com password is stored as "wpw", my ebay.com password is stored as "epw", and under "pw" I store a default password that I use for all the unimportant sites I register for. To log into any site, all I have to do is remember the abbreviation in the bit lever. That's much easier than memorizing dozens of different passwords.

– *Typing HTML phrases:* Techies will find this most useful. I've defined "ahr" to yield "<a href=""></a>", a common chunk of HTML code that sets up a hyperlink. Whether I'm in a text editor or a Web browser's editing window, I can create these key HTML strings quickly and error-free.

A bit lever must work in every application on the computer—from the text editor to the Web browser to the file system. This is why a feature like Microsoft Word's AutoCorrect is insufficient, since it only works in one application. There are many bit levers available, but here are three good, inexpensive options: Mac users can choose between Typinator (available at ergonis.com) or TypeIt4me (available at typeit4me.com), and Windows users can download a bit lever called ActiveWords from activewords.com. (Apple and Microsoft haven't yet built bit levers into their operating systems, but they should.)

The key to using a bit lever is to start slowly, defining a few abbreviation-expansion pairs every week to see what "sticks." Which do you naturally remember? Which do you use a lot? It takes some time to get really effective with a bit lever, but like any good investment, the returns compound over time. In over ten years of using a bit lever, I've built up well over a thousand abbreviation-expansion pairs. I use many of them on a daily basis—to correct a misspelling, retrieve a password, or type some text.

Perhaps the most important aspect of a bit lever is that it invites continual improvement. I'm still adding new expansions so that my typing keeps getting faster and more accurate. Like bit literacy itself, a bit lever works best with long-term practice.

Finally, a word of warning: if you use a bit lever diligently for a few weeks and begin to realize its benefits, you will *never* want to use a machine that doesn't have one. You will resent every Internet cafe PC that stupidly requires you to type every character, and typing on friends' computers will feel impossibly slow. Once you experience improved productivity, you'll never want to go back.

Avoiding the mouse

When using any software application, the bit-literate user should *avoid* using the computer mouse and try to use a keyboard command instead. Like a bit lever, this practice takes time to adopt but can significantly raise your productivity.

This is not to say that the computer mouse is unnecessary; far from it. I often reach for the mouse to root around in the file system, move documents around, or accomplish an obscure task on the computer. The mouse is also a constant necessity online, of course, for clicking links and buttons in the Web browser. But in many common tasks the mouse is much slower than the keyboard. To work most productively, the bit-literate user should keep both hands on the keyboard (fingers resting on home keys), never reaching for the mouse except when the keyboard can't accomplish a task.

The bit-literate ideal is to engage bits at the speed of thought: finding, viewing, creating, editing, sharing, and deleting bits as quickly as your synapses fire. This is an achievable goal if all ten fingers are on the keyboard, but not if one hand is constantly reaching over to grab the mouse. The mouse requires too much physical movement; the keyboard is the fastest, most efficient input device we have.*

In most software applications, common commands are accessible via the keyboard. One example is the Save command, available in most Macintosh applications via the easily-typed command-S keystroke. Windows programs usually assign the Save command to the wrist-contorting combination of control-S. (This, by the way, points to one of Microsoft's all-time biggest user interface blunders. The most common Windows commands rely on the control key, which is located all the way in the lower-left of the keyboard. Like the Qwerty keymap, the control key forces the user's hand to stretch uncomfortably, both slowing down work and increasing wear-and-tear on the wrist. Apple got it right, using the command key adjacent to the space bar, where the user's thumb

---

* This will change someday when brain-computer interfaces, now in their infancy, improve and become more widely available.

can easily reach.* The Mac command key usually is labeled with either a or ⌘.)

Even though it's slower, many people use the mouse, not the keyboard, to save a file. Consider the steps it takes to use the mouse. Unless they know a shortcut, users must...

— take their hand off of the keyboard and reach for the mouse

— move the mouse pointer up to the File menu

— click the mouse

— move the mouse down to the "Save" option

— click the mouse again

— and move their hand back to the keyboard.

That's six steps, including two broad physical movements, just to write some bits to the disk. To call this inefficient is a bit of an understatement. It's like someone who doesn't want to use a key to start their car but instead prefers to open the hood, fiddle about with some wires, hear the car start, close the hood, and then get in the car. If this person drove the car with any frequency, it would be reasonable to expect him to take a minute to learn the easier alternative.

Now consider the one-step alternative to saving a file: type command-S.

And "Save" is just one keystroke that is useful to know. Most applications have several common commands—open, close, cut, copy, paste, and so on—that have keystrokes. (They're usually displayed in the menus; look for them when you drag a menu down

---

* Years ago, a Unix computer from Sun Microsystems offered the only other good alternative I've ever seen: the control key switched places with the Caps Lock, adjacent to the left pinky's home position. Given the importance of the control key, and the unimportance of Caps Lock – itself a throwback to the days of mechanical typewriters – why don't Windows PC manufacturers try this out?

with the mouse.) Why wouldn't every single user use keystrokes? After all, they're easier, faster, more accurate, and physically healthier than the mouse. (Frequent mouse use, like typing in Qwerty, contributes to repetitive stress injury.) Some users may be unaware of the keystrokes, never having been taught; others prefer the mouse because it's more familiar and doesn't require memorizing any keystrokes. Bit-literate users, though, must master the common keyboard commands—and then constantly improve their productivity by finding other ways to use the keyboard instead of the mouse.*

For advanced users: macros

Advanced users should learn how to create macros. A macro is a series of steps—commands, keystrokes, clicks—that users can program into the computer once, and then run many times with a single keystroke. (If you're not sure how to get started, ask the nearest techie—or IT department—for a tutorial on macros; someone may be happy to teach you.) For example, say someone hands you a text file and asks you to "clean up the data" (perhaps to prepare a mail merge or some other task) by deleting the second comma on every line. One way is to do it manually: search twice for a comma, delete, go to the next line; search twice, delete, next line; and so on. But for a file with thousands of lines it would be impossible. A macro, however, could loop these steps into one command, allowing you to execute the process with a single keystroke. Macros can thus turn the keyboard into a bit lever for arbitrarily complex actions.

Some applications, like FileMaker and Excel, have a built-in macro or scripting utility for use on their own files; there are also software tools like QuicKeys (available at quickeys.com for both Mac and Windows) that can run macros in any application. Without

---

* In Mac OSX, System Preferences contains a Keyboard Shortcuts section that allows users to define keystrokes for many commands. QuicKeys software offers the same capability for both Macs and Windows PCs.

macros, users are at the mercy of any repetitive tasks that come their way; with them, they never have to do repetitive work on the computer ever again.

One-touch access

Many users constantly use the mouse to start common applications or switch between them. For example, to start Microsoft Word—a common daily task—many Windows users grab the mouse, click the Start button, then click the Word icon. Switching from Word to the e-mail program requires grabbing the mouse and hunting for the appropriate icon on the task bar (among a slew of icons for other applications, folders, and files in that area of the screen). This is an awful waste of time and energy.

The solution is one-touch access: yet another way to use the keyboard, instead of the mouse, to increase productivity. Bit-literate users must know how to access their favorite applications, folders, and files with a single keystroke.

Setting up these keystrokes is easy with a tool like QuicKeys; the only other requirement is committing to learning and using these keystrokes instead of the mouse. I've set up my computer (and all my employees' computers) to use the following keystrokes for the most common applications:

- F6: word processor (on the Macs at my company, it's AppleWorks)
- F7: Web browser (Safari or Firefox)
- F8: e-mail (Apple Mail or Mailsmith)
- F9: text editor (TextWrangler)
- F10: calendar (Now Up-to-Date)

On a Windows computer the applications would be different— the word processor would most likely be Word, and the e-mail and calendar would probably be Outlook—but the keystrokes could be the same. Function commands, the F keys at the top of the keyboard, are good choices for system-wide keystrokes because they're generally not in use by anything else.* Users should also have one-touch access to commonly used files and folders:

– Files: QuicKeys allows you to define a keystroke to open a given file. This is best for the one or two files that you open most often. For example, at my company we define command-shift-A as the keystroke on everyone's computer that brings up the team address list. No matter what application the user is using at the moment, command-shift-A brings up the address list in the text editor. (Text is the simplest and quickest format for the file; there's no need to hunt around an intranet or bring up a slow-moving database.) To find a coworker's phone number, an employee just types one keystroke and the list pops up instantly.

– Folders: A Mac-based tool called Default Folder (available at defaultfolder.com) allows users to get to any folder in the file system with one keystroke. (Windows users should get a roughly equivalent tool, FileBox eXtender, at hyperionics.com.) For example, to open the parent folder in my computer's file system, I just type command-1. This works whether I'm on the desktop (it pops up the folder window) or inside an application and need to navigate to the folder to save or open a file. Default Folder has saved me countless hours of clicking through the file system to find and open my several most commonly visited folders.

One-touch access also makes it especially quick and easy to share bits between common applications. For example, I may see some text on a Web page that I want to put in a new text file. After selecting the text (this is one action that may require the mouse, though command-A can select everything on the page), I type four keystrokes:

---

* Their existence on the keyboard at all, in fact, is a throwback to the early days when only techies used computers, and computer processors were so weak that having twelve functions available on a single keyboard was really cutting-edge.

- command-C to copy the text
- F9 to go to the text editor
- command-N to create a new file
- command-V to paste in the text

One-touch access makes the task almost instantly achievable. Of course, it requires practice, but typing that sequence of keystrokes is an enormous improvement over using the mouse to navigate to, select, and click the right menu items.

This is how I work with bits at the speed of thought: in my mind I see the bits flowing from the Web page to a new text file, and it just happens. It's important to realize that I'm working directly with the *bits*, not the applications, to get the job done. I keep my mind focused on the bits, and how I'm moving or changing them, but everything else is a blur—applications arrive, quickly play some part, and then move away again. The bits are in focus at all times.

This is peak performance: engaging bits directly, and only using tools in as-needed supporting roles. The goal of bit literacy is to engage the bits as efficiently as possible—ignoring what the applications want you to do, and instead using them for what *you* want to do. Bit literacy is a truly user-centered method: it puts users in charge of their own productivity and frees them from the unnecessary constraints of their tools. Bit-literate users should constantly attempt to reach this level of performance.

Taking screenshots

The easiest way to create image-bits on a computer is to take a screenshot—that is, turn the contents of the screen, or part of the screen, into its own image file. It's like carrying a digital camera wherever you go in the bit world, so that you can take a picture of anything you see there, at any moment, in any application. Screenshots are often useful when using the Web: documenting something you spot on a Web page, saving an online receipt, or making a clipping of an interesting graphic.

Screenshots are easy on Macs and Windows PCs. Macs have offered screenshots for years with the same keystrokes: command-shift-3 takes a shot of the entire screen, and command-shift-4 turns the cursor into crosshairs, allowing the user to select a section of the screen to save as an image. Windows computers have the PrntScrn button, which places a screenshot on the clipboard, available to then be pasted into a Word document. (There are also screenshot applications—Print Screen Deluxe for Windows and Snapz Pro for Macintosh, among others—that offer increased functionality.)

Backup

There are two kinds of users: those who already back up, and those who will. I've heard different versions of this quote over the years—I'm not sure who originated it—but it's absolutely true. The users most enthusiastic about learning how to back up their files are those who have just lost all of their data, due to a hard drive crash or a stolen laptop. Bit-literate users need not wait until disaster strikes; working responsibly with bits means making backups.

Users in a large corporate environment might be able to rely on the internal technology department to handle backups, though it's good to confirm that those backups do occur. Other users should buy an external hard drive that's big enough to contain several times the memory of the computer's hard drive. Users should then back up their data on the external hard drive every week or two.

To make a backup, create a folder on the top level of the external hard drive, and name the folder with the current date. (There's no need to include the word "backup" in the folder name, since that's redundant; everything on the external hard drive is a backup.) Then drag in all the contents of your computer that you want to back up. The backup can take an hour or more, slowing down other applications in the process, so it may be best to run the backup overnight. (In such cases, be sure not to leave the room until you see the data starting to transfer; occasionally a window pops up asking a question before the backup gets started.) If the hard drive is full, delete the oldest folder or two, empty the trash, and then start the backup.

Remember that the external hard drive can also crash, even at the same moment that your laptop crashes. A lightning strike or a worse disaster, like a fire or flood, can affect all electronic equipment under the same roof. Thus it's important to have an even more secure backup plan to complement the external drive. One solution is to burn a set of DVDs of all your bits once or twice a year and store them in a different location. (Make sure to use a permanent marker to write the date of the backup on each disk, so they're easy to distinguish later.)

There's one other essential backup tool that every bit-literate user should know: e-mail. To make a daily backup of your few most important files, just e-mail them as attachments to a free online e-mail account such as Yahoo Mail or Gmail. This is faster and easier than backing up to an external hard drive, and you can do it from anywhere. It also ensures that the data is stored in a different physical location from your computer and external hard drive. Just remember that you've then turned the bits over to another company to host, and if you're concerned with privacy you may want to examine the company's privacy policy before you send the bits there.

Discernment: choosing the right application

The chapter on file formats discussed the importance of working with simple file formats. Applications are similar; it's important to choose the simplest, most appropriate tool for the job. Here are some guidelines:

– For any task involving words, a text editor is usually the best choice of application, unless there's a specific need for something else. For example, as discussed earlier, a contacts file is best maintained as an ASCII text file rather than in a proprietary, complex address book program. For text that needs to be e-mailed, it's usually best to write and send the text in the body of an e-mail, not as an attachment.

- For files with complex data (like name, phone, address, e-mail, and other fields) that need to be sorted in various ways, a database program is more appropriate than a text editor. FileMaker is the best choice for both Mac and Windows users. (Avoid using Microsoft Access, which is a poorly designed database program. And as described below, also avoid using Microsoft Excel for databases.)

- Tasks involving lots of calculations require a spreadsheet, which is essentially a programmable calculator displayed in grid format. Microsoft Excel is the dominant tool and file format, though Google Spreadsheet is a free alternative (and is compatible with Excel). One common mistake with Excel, however, is to use it as a database. You might as well use Microsoft Word to compose music, or use Outlook to create a slideshow. Excel was built as a spreadsheet, not a database, and so it should be used for calculations, formulas, and the like—but not managing a database.

- Another application that bit-literate users must be familiar with is Google. The popular website offers a set of essential applications reaching far beyond its well-known search feature. For example, the Google search bar can act as a calculator (type "135 * 329" and it responds with "44 415"), a currency converter (type "1 usd to euro" to get the current rate), a weather forecaster (type "weather" and a zip code to get the local forecast), a UPS and FedEx package tracker (search on the tracking number), and other functions. There are many other useful, free applications available via the "more" link on the Google home page.

One final note about applications: when using a new application, users should always begin by seeing what they can customize in the application's appearance and behavior—particularly to turn off distracting or irritating interface features. Windows users should look for Customize and Options screens; Mac users should look for Preferences. (In Microsoft Word, users should also turn off any unnecessary features they see on the AutoCorrect screen.) This customization is available for operating systems, too. Mac users, for example, should use System Preferences, available under the Apple menu, to customize the overall look and feel of the computer. (The choice of which operating system to use—Mac or Windows—is covered in Appendix B.)

Text functions

As described in the chapter on file formats, text files are best created in a text editor—not Microsoft Word—in part because a text editor offers several special text-oriented functions. The bit-literate user should know how to use these functions whenever working in a text editor:

–   *Wrapping and unwrapping:*
    Line breaks often creep into text in strange places, as when copying text from a
    website and then pasting it into an e-mail, text file, or elsewhere. Just as
    in this example, in which the paragraph text breaks in different places, it
    can be laborious to manually have to go back and delete the line breaks to make the text wrap correctly.

    Most text editors have a feature ("Unwrap Lines" or "Remove Line Breaks") that will instantly clean up that text. Bit-literate users should know that feature and its converse, which "wraps" lines by inserting line breaks after a certain number of characters. For example, if a line of text should be no more than 68 characters (and this is the recommended maximum length of any line in plaintext e-mail), then the "Hard Wrap" feature will take care of it.

–   *Search and replace:* Many users know how to search for given text in a Word file. Users should also know how to find and replace all instances in a file, or even across a set of files in a given folder. A good text editor should also allow users to search backwards, turn on and off case-sensitivity, and tweak the search in other ways. Users should be familiar with these options in the text editor's "Search" or "Find" command.

— *Character count:* Users should know how to count the lines and characters in any text file, *and* in any span of highlighted text within the file. (In TextWrangler this is available via the "Get Info" command, but other text editors may call it something different.)

— *Change case:* Users should be familiar with the "Change Case" (or equivalent) feature, for changing a range of text to ALL CAPITALS, all lower case, or Capitalized Words Only.

— *Educating and dumbing down quotes:* Users should know the difference between "smart quotes" and more ASCII-friendly "dumb quotes" and be able to change an entire file from one to the other. (Similarly, users should also know smart apostrophes from ASCII apostrophes, also known as hash marks: here's a smart apostrophe, and here's a hash mark.) This is usually available via an "Educate Quotes" feature in the text editor.

— *Opening non-text files:* Any good text editor can open a non-ASCII file, like a Word document, and show all the data inside (as demonstrated in the file formats chapter). Users should know how to do this with the Open File command.

Basic image editing

The photos chapter covered how to organize a photo bitstream, but users should also know how to make basic edits to individual files. These are akin to the basic text-editing functions that all computer users learn—adding, selecting, editing, and deleting words. Strangely, most users are never taught the equivalent skills in photos; this is unfortunate, as digital images are becoming more prevalent and important in users' day-to-day lives.

These are the basic image-editing functions that all bit-literate users should know:

- cropping
- changing brightness and contrast
- resizing
- adding simple elements like lines, circles, and text to the image—for example, to highlight a certain element
- e-mailing one or more images

These are all easy skills to learn, and they don't require an expensive tool like Photoshop. All but one, in fact, are included in popular and free photo tools like iPhoto and Picasa. (The exception is adding simple elements, which is easily done with GraphicConverter, included for free on many Macs, and most Windows paint programs.) Resizing and e-mailing images need some extra explanation, though, since they are increasingly common operations for the average user.

Resizing an image is mainly important when e-mailing photos. Digital cameras with five or more megapixels create huge image files, and attaching multiple photos to a single e-mail may make the e-mail too big for recipients' inboxes to accept. (And depending on the recipients' image-viewing software, the images may be too large to view easily on the screen.) Thus it's important to understand the difference between full-sized and e-mail-sized images.

Full-sized images, the original files from the camera, are mostly useful for printing, since they have such high resolution.* But they're not appropriate for e-mailing, since they're so big. Unless

---

* A five-megapixel camera can create images at a resolution of 2,560 pixels by 1,920 pixels; that's enough resolution to make photo-quality prints at eleven by sixteen inches—much larger than the standard four- by six-inch snapshot print. *Two* megapixels are all that's necessary to create good snapshot prints. As *New York Times* columnist David Pogue wrote, "The Megapixel Myth ... goes like this: 'The more megapixels a camera has, the better the pictures.' It's a big fat lie. The camera companies and camera stores all know it, but they continue to exploit our misunderstanding...." ("Breaking the Myth of Megapixels," the *New York Times*, February 8, 2007.)

the recipient wants to print out the photos, there's no need to send full-sized images. Instead, to prepare photos for e-mailing, resize them to either 800 by 600 pixels, or 640 by 480 pixels. (On the Mac, iPhoto makes this process really easy: just click "Email", then choose "Medium" in the size menu that pops up.) This guarantees that the e-mail won't be too big for recipients, and that the images will be displayed in an appropriate size.

It's also important to use a descriptive Subject line when e-mailing photos. There's no need to rename the photo files from their original camera-assigned names (like "DSC01325.JPG"), but the Subject line should communicate to recipients what the photos are about. And be sure to filter the photos beforehand (as described in the managing photos chapter), so that you send only the best, non-duplicate shots. Be empathetic to the recipient by sending the fewest shots that communicate what the event was about.

Finally, you may prefer to avoid e-mailing photos altogether and instead upload the pictures to an online photo-sharing website. Such sites automatically resize the images to display nicely on the Web page, and there's no danger of filling up recipients' e-mail inboxes. However, these sites often require recipients to create an account and endure distracting advertisements just to see your photos. These irritations may make it less likely that recipients will bother to look at your photos. Especially if you have only a few photos to share, e-mailing resized images may be the best option.

Saving bookmarks

Bit-literate users should stay on the lookout for tools and online resources that can help them improve their skills. This isn't referring to "productivity blogs" that gush about the latest tips and tricks, or technology-worship sites that lavish praise on the newest, shiniest gadgets. Rather, users should watch for the rare site or tool that offers something genuinely useful for getting a job done.

Whenever they find such a resource, users should save a pointer to the site in a bookmark.

All Web browsers have a bookmarks, or "favorites," feature that allows users to store links to their favorite sites. It's useful to have a handful of your most-visited sites saved this way in the browser, for easy access. However, it's common to come across a site (or individual page) that you only *might* want to get back to some other time. In these situations it's best to use an online bookmarks service. My favorite is del.icio.us (also available at delicious.com); furl.net is a popular alternative. Sign up for a (free) account on one of these services and save your bookmarks there, adding tags, or keywords, to each bookmark so that you can find it again later. This is one situation where tags are genuinely valuable.

For example, I recently bookmarked (in my del.icio.us account) a Web page showing how to create images in the Pop Art cartoon style of Roy Lichtenstein. I won't access this page frequently, and I may never look it up again, but if some time in the future I think, "Whatever happened to that Roy Lichtenstein thing?", I can click into the "art" tag in my del.icio.us bookmarks—or search for "pop art" or "lichtenstein"—and the link will come up. Also, by storing these bookmarks on a website, I can access them from any computer—not just my own.

Playing games

I've saved the best for last: games. For years I've maintained "Good Experience Games," a list of well-designed, fun, free games that I've come across online. (Find it at www.goodexperience.com/games.) This is for more than amusement; each game exhibits an interface element, or some aspect of the user experience, that is worth experiencing and learning from. Game play is a great teacher about what works and doesn't work in online experiences and user interfaces. While it's not productive to sink endless hours into a game, it can be relaxing—and instructive—to occasionally take a break for a few minutes of game play.

Future additions

Users who master these "other essentials" and all the methods of previous chapters will be bit-literate, or close to it—working more productively, and in a healthier way, than they ever have before. But no list can account for every possible skill necessary in every possible context. The technology world changes fast, and there will surely be new essentials added to this list in the coming years—even as the basic philosophy and goals of bit literacy remain the same.

Chapter 13: **The Future of Bit Literacy**

The age of bits has just begun. Bits are taking on massive importance in our lives and work, and they have only just arrived. In such early days it's hard to grasp even the *scope* of the changes that are occurring, let alone meet the challenges themselves. This makes bit literacy especially important, because bits will change the world more quickly than we might like.

Imagine you could graph the number of e-mails you receive on a given day. (This would be a good feature for a future bit-literate e-mail program.) If the graph showed the past five years, it would almost certainly slope upwards. For most users it would look like a classic "hockey stick" graph, with a rapidly rising curve ending in a near-vertical slope. The obvious question is, where does it go from here?

Consider what will happen in five, ten, or twenty years, as bits increase exponentially in the e-mail inbox, on the Web, and on phones and PDAs and other devices. Without proper training, users everywhere will face an increasingly urgent problem of overload. *Now* is the moment to learn bit literacy. It's like getting in shape on a slow-moving treadmill before it speeds up to a sprinting pace.

The future will also bring new, unfamiliar bitstreams that users will be expected to create, maintain, and receive from others. This has happened before. Twenty years ago my parents hadn't heard of e-mail, and now they're expected to use an e-mail account, daily, to communicate with children and grandchildren, as well as friends and neighbors. Basic e-mail skills are now a social necessity for many people—but e-mail is not the last major bitstream that will arise. What bitstream will we have to master in future years that we haven't heard of today?

A prime candidate, almost certainly coming soon to many users, is the bitstream of "life bits." Several universities and companies (notably, Microsoft) have already started research and development of the technology. New devices will record every moment of the user's day, every day. A mobile phone today can record a few minutes of audio, and a digital camera can take a few still images or a small amount of video; the life bitstream will be on *all* the time, and it will be recorded by a device that's easy to carry—or wear—without attracting undue notice. The camera could be embedded in an everyday object, like a mobile phone. As *The Economist* recently put it, "In a decade's time a typical phone will have enough storage capacity to be able to video its user's entire life ... such 'life records' will be used for everything from security to settling accident claims with insurance firms."*

The life bitstream will raise new and important issues. Should it be socially acceptable, for example, to record a private conversation with a friend? How will anyone be sure that they're *not* being recorded, in public or private? Storage and organization will also pose challenges for users. The sheer size of the bitstream boggles the mind; managing a photo library over several years will look trivial by comparison. The discipline of "letting the bits go" will be essential.

Most importantly, new bitstreams will raise issues of ownership. Whichever company releases the first LifeBits product will want to mediate users' access to their life bits. Bit-literate users will know better than to fall in line and use the tool exactly as directed. I'm not predicting a grim Orwellian scenario, just noting that the user's long-term interest is rarely the same as the corporation's.

Ownership of bits is already an issue today, and it will become increasingly important. As discussed previously, many file formats (notably, for music) now come with DRM, or "digital rights management," built in to prevent the user from having direct, unfettered access to the bits. Depending on one's point of view,

---

* "The phone of the future," *The Economist*, December 2, 2006.

DRM is either a necessary tool in the enforcement of copyright law, or a gratuitous attempt by corporations to control what their customers do with purchased products.* Either way, users should be aware of this as a bit-literate issue. Bits are truly owned by the user only when they're...

- stored on the user's own hardware, not on someone else's website

- accessible via the file system, not locked up in an application

- saved in a non-proprietary, DRM-free format like ASCII, not a proprietary format like Word.

Some companies have begun leasing access to bitstreams like music and videos, without allowing any copying. This may be attractive to some users, but they should be aware of the significant difference between leasing temporary access to bits and owning them.

The future will also bring more combinations of bits and the physical environment. Global Positioning System (GPS) data is a good example: some mobile phones today can transmit their exact geographical location to another user or post it on the Web. Parents of young users can then open a bitstream of geo-location data showing where their children are at every moment, even setting alarms in the event that they stray outside a predetermined area. Bit-literate parents will have to choose whether to add their child's location-bitstream to their media diet. Children may be the most affected of all. How will it change their experience of childhood to know that they are being tracked, to the meter, every waking minute?

GPS data isn't the only trail of bits that people will generate in the physical world. Satellite cameras are getting more and more accurate, and any moment you walk outside, you (or your car) could be photographed for the next update of Google Earth.

---

* One organization that fights corporate abuse of copyright law is the EFF, or Electronic Frontier Foundation, at eff.org.

(Knowing this, some companies and activists have cleverly painted enormous logos and slogans on roofs and other flat expanses visible to satellites.) Cameras will be nearly ubiquitous on street level, too, at least in urban areas. Corporations, police, even friends with "life recorders" will capture the actions and utterances of everyone in sight, whether they like it or not.

Tracking data will increase in the online world, too. Users leave a digital trail showing where they go and what they do online, and companies will continue to invest in mining that data. (Users can turn off cookies and other tracking mechanisms, but doing so often requires special skills.) Only a minority of users will be very concerned about their privacy online. Most users would prefer to eliminate the frustrations and complexity of technology, even with a loss in privacy. Bit overload, not privacy, will be their primary concern.

As bits increase, new kinds of tools will become more important. Information visualization software will promise to display large data sets for easy scanning, and "social software" like blogs and wikis will offer users new ways to collaborate online. A few instances of these tools will succeed, but many more will fail.[1] Ultimately, though, tools will play only a supporting role. The pertinent question is whether individual users will commit to learning and practicing bit literacy.

Bit literacy in offices, companies, governments

Bit literacy will greatly affect the office. Employers, regardless of whether they use the term "bit literacy," will expect productivity in the increasingly digital office.[2] (Employees who can survive, and

---

1 In the December 3, 2006 *New York Times Magazine* article "Open Source Spying," by Clive Thompson, NYU professor Clay Shirky put it best: "The normal case for social software is failure."

2 The "paperless office" may also be within reach, at last, for some companies. As employees become more effective with bits, they will have less need to print out e-mails, documents, and other files. Paper will always be useful in some situations, but bit-literate users will avoid it when possible.

thrive, in the daily tsunami of e-mails and todos will be hired, promoted, and rewarded. Ineffective, stressed employees who don't reply to e-mails and leave todos undone will be left behind. The old excuse "I get too much e-mail" won't be worth much when the coworker across the hall works faster and more accurately under the same load.

The same dynamic will decide the fate of companies and entire industries. Any team's ability to manage its bits could make the difference between success and failure. This trend has already begun. It's easy to spot today's most productive, efficient companies, because they're in the lead. For example, Google has built its company culture, and thus its products, with bit-literate values of speed and simplicity; by any measure it is one of the most successful technology companies in history. There are productivity gains available to *any* company that trains its staff to be bit-literate. Companies that simply "go with the flow," and invest where their technology vendors tell them to, will lag behind.

Governments will also have to engage bits better, on all levels, or suffer the consequences. Bit literacy is already emerging as an issue of national security in the U.S., where traditionally paper-based spy agencies are under mounting pressure to detect terrorist threats using software that tracks online activity and other bitstreams. The *New York Times Magazine* recently quoted a young analyst complaining about "mountains of information, and no way to organize it."*

The biggest question is how bit-literate users will change the technology industry. There are many improvements they may press for: better user interfaces, more direct access to their bits, less proprietary file formats, and more reliable tools that don't require buying an "upgrade" every two or three years. Bits should be accessible and manageable by everyone who wants them. By using and buying only the most bit-literate tools, and not purchasing

---

* "Open Source Spying," by Clive Thompson, the *New York Times Magazine*, December 3, 2006.

others, users may finally bring about a change in an industry that has such potential to improve people's lives. First, though, users must learn and practice the discipline.

The future belongs to bit-literate users. The world will continue to change, bringing new bitstreams, new devices, and new challenges. By any measure of productivity or health, bit-literate users will benefit the most. And that makes it a bright future, no matter what changes occur. The next upgrade, the next buzzword, the next fad all come and go, but the user stays. Bit literacy will remain, too: a discipline that invites users to let the bits go, in order to work more productively and live fuller, healthier lives.

Appendix A: **Message to Developers**

As important as bit literacy is for the future of technology users, it's even more important for developers. Users will increasingly demand, and buy, bit-literate tools—of which there are nearly none today. The market opportunity is enormous. Consider the few bit-literate tools available to users today:

- One todo list (Gootodo.com)

- Few calendar programs (Now Up-to-Date for the Mac; Google Calendar for all platforms)

- Several text editors (TextWrangler for the Mac, for example) that are mostly optimized for programmers' needs

- Two photo-management tools (Picasa for Windows and iPhoto for Mac)

- Not a single e-mail program (The industry should be embarrassed by its lack of progress. Claris Emailer v1, released in 1996 for the Mac, is superior to most e-mail programs today. I know of no bit-literate e-mail programs ever made in Windows, and no online e-mail service today is fully bit-literate.)

It wouldn't take much to fill this market need. All it requires is properly trained developers and a little bit of time; no expensive, high-tech features are necessary. In fact, many existing tools could be improved greatly by adding a few low-tech, easily implemented features, and removing or hiding unnecessary, distracting features that are irrelevant to most users.

Bit-literate developers must design tools that invite users to become bit-literate themselves. Such a tool must be empathetic to users' level of expertise when they begin using it, yet still offer a path toward future growth.

We can thus state two complementary guidelines for bit-literate development:

1. Always, in all cases, "first things first": make basic tasks the easiest and quickest to perform, and display the most important information most prominently, while hiding secondary information and advanced features (which only a minority of advanced users will seek out). "First things first" allows all users to start using a tool as quickly and easily as possible, attaining immediate benefits from the tool with the least investment of time and energy.

2. At the same time, give users a way to continually improve their productivity: invite them to invest more in order to gain more. This means offering bit-literate features, options, and preferences that allow users to work better, faster, and more accurately, if they wish to do so.

With those two guidelines in mind, below are some more specific feature requests.

Bit-literate tools should...

– *Set better defaults.* The factory settings of any tool should be the ones that are in the long-term interest of the user. Marketing departments sometimes set defaults in the company's favor, or "what we can get away with without the users noticing." This is shameful. Every default setting, like the application itself, must be genuinely helpful to the user; otherwise it's not bit-literate. Moreover, defaults should be oriented to the majority of normal users—not techies—so that the tool is immediately usable by the biggest group of people.

– *Provide more ways to delete bits.* To "let the bits go," bit-literate users will want to delete their bits, or at least move them out of the incoming location, in lots of different ways. The Delete feature will be especially important, and it should also be combined with other features where appropriate. For example, a bit-literate e-mail program must offer "delete-and-next," a single command that deletes the current message and advances to the next one. (There must be a "delete-and-previous," too.) Other deletion features may work automatically, like the time window, described below.

— *Offer more time-based features.* Many bitstreams are best organized by time; tools that operate on those bitstreams should be designed with that in mind. For example, a bit-literate e-mail program might show how many messages arrived in the inbox in the past month, and how many messages were still in the inbox every day at midnight. (Graphs work well in displaying time-based data and should be liberally available, always with an easily accessed option for users to close or hide them.) There are other time-based features listed below.

  • *The time window:* This enables deleted bits to stay in a holding location before being automatically erased from memory after a certain time period. This allows users to use Delete liberally, without fear of accidentally erasing something important. For example, an e-mail program should allow the user to set a time window for the number of days that messages in the "trash" will be kept before the program erases them. A time window also allows users to avoid unbounded bitstreams by capping the amount of data that can accumulate. For example, by setting a window of a week on a Sent Items folder, users can retrieve anything they sent in the past week, and they never have to clean out the folder. Time windows are useful in many more applications than e-mail; for starters, Mac OSX's Trash and the Windows Recycling Bin should offer time windows. (Currently these tools allow users only two options—to keep everything, or delete everything all at once—but bit-literate users may prefer to automatically delete all files older than a certain number of days.)

- *Future forwarding:* This allows users to forward bits into the future. The idea was pioneered by Gootodo.com, the first bit-literate todo list, which allows users to e-mail todos to future days. It's the converse of the time window; instead of deleting bits after a certain amount of time, future forwarding *hides* bits for a certain duration before bringing them back to the user's attention.

- *Time-based filing:* Tools should get better at filing bits by user-defined time periods. Despite its many features, iPhoto has no two-level storage system and thus requires a separate application—iPhoto Library—to set one up artificially. iPhoto, Picasa, and other relevant applications should give users full control over the time periods in which they file their bits. (Automated filing is not the answer. iPhoto can automatically organize photos by time, but only based on the metadata encoded in the photos. But metadata can be wrong, as in the case of a scanned image of a much older item.)

- *Timeout:* Some bitstreams should have finite life spans by default and require active, manual renewal after a certain duration or number of iterations. Today's tools allow users only one way to open a new bitstream: subscribing forever until the user actively unsubscribes. (For example, an RSS feed lasts until it's deleted.) Tools should allow some bitstreams to lapse after a certain time, and then remind the user to renew if they wish.

— *Allow advanced users to change non-essential defaults.* A few years ago Mac OSX made anti-aliased text the standard across all its applications, and it removed the option for users to change the setting. As a result, users are now forced to view blurry text in applications like Safari and FileMaker whether they like it or not. Similarly irritating are the cartoon animations in OSX that play when some windows are opened or minimized. The machine's response time to keyboard commands can be delayed by a second or two as interface elements fly around the screen.

It's a drain on productivity. These features are OK to offer as *options*—even as default settings—as long as advanced users have the option to disable them. Stated another way, it's fine to add training wheels to a tool, as long as they're removable.

— *Offer ASCII-friendly features.* Tools should be able to import and export ASCII data without complaining. (In contrast, creating a text file in Word and attempting to save it in .txt format brings up a popup that warns the user about "formatting or password" features possibly being lost—even though the file contains only ASCII characters.*) Proprietary formats may be unavoidable in some tools, but wherever possible, users must have an easily accessed option to work with open formats like ASCII.

— *Make common features keyboard-accessible.* For example, in an e-mail program, the user should be able to open an e-mail, write a reply (either quoting or not quoting the original message, and either replying to all or just the sender), and send it, all without ever touching the mouse. Of course, applications should still allow users to access features and menus via the mouse, but users should have the *option* to pursue higher productivity by using the keyboard.

— *Stop gratuitous attempts to lock in market share.* There are many examples of this user-hostile practice in the technology industry, but the most prominent are probably Microsoft Windows and Microsoft Office, which are "upgraded" every few years. Previous versions are usually incompatible with the upgrade, which pressures users to buy the new version. This makes Microsoft a lot of money, but it forces Microsoft developers to constantly invent new features that may not be necessary or relevant to users. Thus each upgrade tends to be slower, more bloated, and harder to use than the last version. This does little good for users, and it only works for Microsoft while its market remains non-competitive. On the other hand, Microsoft (or any other company) could win millions of enthusiastic customers

---

* Popup text from Microsoft Word 2004 for Mac, version 11.0.

worldwide by releasing new productivity tools that are designed for the long-term interest of the users, not the short-term interests of the company.

The above list is not exhaustive. Bit-literate developers must continually seek more ways to help users delete, defer, skip, omit, and in general let the bits go. In doing so, they will allow users to work in freer, healthier, and more productive ways.

Bit literacy is not a fanciful or unattainable ideal for developers to work toward. To the contrary, it's a principled philosophy that should inform design, engineering, and management at all levels. (It should start early, with universities teaching bit literacy to young engineers and designers as the new paradigm.) Developers should make bit literacy available to all users. No developer or tool should deny users a way to improve their productivity, and no company should prevent developers from working for the long-term best interest of their users. Bit-literate development is simply the *right* way to make technology today.

In the long run, though, bit literacy will likely be adopted by the technology industry because it's good business. Applications that treat their users best will, in the long run, win in their respective markets—as long as those markets are competitive. (In a monopoly or other non-competitive environment, the rule works in reverse; companies that lock in users tend to dominate, until the market inevitably opens up.) Bit literacy primarily works in favor of the individual user, but by extension it's also in favor of the corporations that serve users well. Companies operating with a long-term, user-centered mindset can be wildly successful by embracing bit literacy.

Appendix B: **On Mac vs. Windows**

At various points in this book I reference Microsoft Windows and Macintosh OSX, the two dominant operating systems today, and suggest tools and methods that are compatible with each operating system. But I never state an explicit recommendation for either operating system. I will do so now, citing Macintosh as the best choice, but I must first qualify my recommendation.

Let me first state that I am not "pro" or "anti" any technology company—Microsoft, Apple, Google, or any other. In evaluating or recommending a tool, my sole concern is users' ability to engage bits in a productive and healthy manner. If a tool allows users to practice bit literacy, I'll recommend it, no matter which company created it. (I have very little interest in the technology industry's politics and fads, which already get enough commentary elsewhere.)

As it happens, though, most tools I recommend happen *not* to be made by Microsoft. The best text editor, todo list, calendar program, word processor, photo manager, music manager, Web browser, search engine, and operating system—among others—are all made by competitors to Microsoft. By some dynamic of their corporate cultures and the larger marketplace, these companies have managed to deliver more bit-literate tools. Microsoft could change, though, and I hope it does. If and when Microsoft begins developing bit-literate tools, I'll happily recommend them.

In the meantime, the question remains for many users: should they buy Windows or Mac? The debate has raged for years, and my words won't be the last on the subject, but I can say confidently that Macintosh is almost always the better choice.

First, the exceptions. There are two situations in which I actually recommend Windows over Macintosh:

1. Some users need to plug into an existing Windows network at school or work, and so Windows is the best choice. Even though a Mac might work perfectly well on the network, the typical IT department will refuse to support Macs; there's no use in fighting them, since they control the network. The user needs to be on good terms with them, anyway, in case their Windows PC has problems later.

2. Some people really are pro-Microsoft and anti-Apple, and they're reflexively opposed to anything Macintosh-related. If the user is one of these people, I immediately agree with their choice of Windows, since they wouldn't be happy with a Mac. (Employees at my company, however, have no choice: regardless of their stance, they all must use our Mac-based "Good Easy" system, described below.)

Now, with exceptions done, we can state the two main reasons to choose a Mac over Windows:

1. Macs are easier to use.

For years Apple has fostered a corporate culture focused on design and innovation. (Apple created the iPod; Microsoft created the animated paper clip.) It's no secret that Microsoft often "borrows" design ideas from Apple for use in its new products. Needless to say, the original versions are better designed. Apple's commitment to the user experience has, over the years, cemented the Mac's position as the easier-to-use computer.

One other advantage is that Apple designed both hardware and software in the Macintosh, creating a more stable, more tightly integrated machine. Microsoft, on the other hand, built Windows on top of an archaic program called DOS, and then had to make it all work with various hardware manufacturers. Because it was built in so many pieces, Windows is unstable and often frustrating to work with. Anyone who has installed a printer or other external device on both Mac and Windows can attest: things "just work" on the Mac, while Windows tends to need a lot of high-tech twiddling (some would call it babysitting) in order to work properly.

Bit literacy allows users to work more productively with less stress, and so it only makes sense to choose the easier-to-use platform. Given the choice between getting things done more or less easily, why would anyone choose the harder option?

2. Macs are more secure against viruses.

Windows PCs are constantly vulnerable to Internet viruses, which pose a constant risk to everything on the user's computer: e-mail, documents, photos, everything. (Microsoft Outlook is particularly vulnerable to viruses, in part because it's such a widespread tool.) In fact, studies have shown that an unprotected PC on the Internet today will be infected by a virus, on average, within fifteen minutes.* In contrast, Macs have very little risk of catching an Internet virus. Fewer viruses are written for Macs, and as stated above, OSX is more stable than Windows and thus less susceptible.

Finally, note that many Macs today can also run Windows, identical to any Windows PC, via software called BootCamp. This can be valuable for users who want to work on a Mac but occasionally have to use a Windows application.

Except for large corporations that are saddled with Windows-based enterprise software, I recommend that companies and individuals standardize on Macintosh computers. They are slightly more expensive in the initial purchase price, but in the long term the combination of Macs and bit literacy training pays a tremendously high return in productivity gains. For a case study, I offer my own company, Creative Good, a ten-year-old consulting firm that issues Macs to all employees. Almost all of our clients

---

* The SANS Internet Storm Center monitors the average "survival time" of a Windows PC at http://isc.sans.org/survivaltime.html.

are Windows-based companies, but we have no trouble sharing files and executing detailed projects. The Mac allows the team to practice bit literacy in e-mail and todo management, file formats, and file management; doing so in Windows would be possible, but more difficult.

The Good Easy

At Creative Good, we never use Macs as they arrive in the box. Before we hand a new Mac to a new employee, we outfit it with something we call the "Good Easy."[1] This is our in-house version of bit literacy, our own particular blend of tools, features, and settings that we use to optimize our computers for the consulting work we do.[2] To any experienced employee at Creative Good, an out-of-the-box Macintosh is painfully inefficient compared to what it becomes after the Good Easy setup.

Separately, whenever we hire a new employee, we set aside time for several sessions of "Good Easy training." This includes many of the methods described in this book, but it's customized to our consulting work and internal processes. (Indeed, any company would have to customize its bit literacy training to its own processes, deciding which skills to focus on and which exceptions to allow.)

---

1 The name was coined by Helen Moriarty, mother of my business partner Phil Terry, back in 1999.

2 Here's most of what we add: QuicKeys for one-touch access to applications and the team contacts file; Default Folder for one-touch folder access; Typinator or TypeIt4Me as the bit lever; TextWrangler as the text editor; AppleWorks as the word processor and wireframing tool; FileMaker for databases; Now Up-to-Date for the calendar; Firefox or Safari as the Web browser; a Gootodo.com account for the todo list; Mailsmith for the e-mail program; Microsoft Office for compatibility to client files; and for really dedicated learners, the Dvorak keymap for the keyboard. We also add Classic Menu and ASM for the upper-left and upper-right menus that were so effective in OS9 but disappeared in OSX. We disable Apple's poorly-designed Spotlight feature and give users the choice of Quicksilver and EasyFind as a replacement.

Whether it's the Good Easy or some other in-house blend, the important thing is to have both a training program and a supporting technology environment to ensure that users can learn and practice bit literacy as a long-term discipline.

Afterword by Phil Terry

Bit literacy may bring about the biggest productivity jump in the global economy over the next twenty years. Millions of people today are overwhelmed and frustrated by the gap between the promise of technology and what they are actually able to achieve using it. There is tremendous opportunity for improvement: most companies ignore the fact that their managers, employees, and customers have no idea how to manage digital information. I commonly witness executives, even at technology firms, flail in their attempts to accomplish simple tasks, like finding documents they have previously created. Inboxes with thousands of e-mails, file structures that make no sense, and other inefficient practices described in this book are common throughout the corporate world.

For the past twenty years, the PC and the Internet have brought dramatic productivity enhancements, helping to keep inflation low, increase corporate profits, and raise wages in some industries. But these technologies have generated more bits, making people more and more overwhelmed. The paradox is that the early success of digital technology in improving productivity is now leading to *less* productivity.

The productivity problem is becoming visible. The *Wall Street Journal* reported recently that the productivity rates of the last decade are indeed slowing, and there is now concern that most executives don't know how to reignite them: "The latest productivity numbers extend a trend that has led many on Wall Street and in academia to wonder whether the U.S. can keep boosting its productivity as much as it has in the recent past."* What this

---

* "Pause Stirs Concern That Growth In Productivity May Be Flattening," by Mark Whitehouse and Tim Aeppel, the *Wall Street Journal,* November 3, 2006.

article misses—along with every other report—is that there *is* a way to increase the productivity rate again. This time, however, it won't come from investing in new technology, but rather from working with and leveraging existing technology in a new way. Bit literacy is the answer: it can raise productivity for a company or an entire industry, as much as it can for an individual worker.

Almost ten years ago, Mark took me up on the challenge to turn bit literacy from his personal tool into an approach accessible to everyone. For several years Mark and I have taught bit literacy to our employees at Creative Good, and we've measured significant results. Based on our annual measures of productivity, we have *doubled* the effectiveness of our employees, even as their level of overload has decreased.

Now it's up to you. Use this book to apply the methods of bit literacy. Let us know how it goes, and feel free to contact us for help.

E-mail Mark and me at comments@bitliteracy.com. We look forward to hearing from you.

Phil Terry
CEO, Creative Good
New York City
www.creativegood.com

More resources: www.bitliteracy.com